FAMILY, FREEDOM, AND FAITH

FAMILY, FREEDOM, AND FAITH

Building Community Today

PAULA M. COOEY

Westminster John Knox Press
Louisville, Kentucky

Book design by Jennifer K. Cox
Cover design by Kim Wohlenhaus

First edition

Published by Westminster John Knox Press
Louisville, Kentucky

This book is printed on acid-free paper that meets the American National Standards Institute Z39.48 standard. ⊗

PRINTED IN THE UNITED STATES OF AMERICA

96 97 98 99 00 01 02 03 04 05 — 10 9 8 7 6 5 4 3 2 1

Library of Congress Cataloging-in-Publication Data

Cooey, Paula M., date–
    Family, freedom, and faith : building community today / Paula M.
Cooey. — 1st ed.
        p.   cm.
    Includes bibliographical references.
    ISBN 0-664-25663-5 (alk. paper)
    1. Church and state—United States.   2. Family—Government
policy—United States.   3. Family—United States.   4. Conservatism—
Religious aspects—Christianity—Controversial literature.
5. Christianity and politics—History—20th century.   6. Family—
United States—Religious life.   7. United States—Religion—1960–   .
I. Title.
BR516.C695   1996   96-276
261.8'3585'0973—dc20

*For Polly, Starr, and Billy
and in memory of Bill*

Contents

Preface   ix
Introduction   1

PART 1: CREATED IN THE IMAGE OF GOD   9

1. Images of the Family   11

Family as Cultural and Political Battleground   12
What Counts as Family?   14
  Biblical Images of the Family   17
  Literary Images of the Family   22
Conclusion   27

2. Family as the People of God   30

What Do Family Values Value?   31
  Religious Activism in the Political Arena   31
  Political Exploitation of Family Values   33
Who Gets to Decide?   35
  Two Different Views of Democracy   37
  The People of Faith and the People of God   40
Conclusion   41

3. Thinking Difference Differently   43

Genesis 2:4–3:24 and Difference   43
Genesis and Gender   46
  The Fatherhood of Men and
    the Motherhood of Everybody   47
  Difference versus Division   55
Thinking Difference   58
  Demonizing the Other   61
  Erasing the Pain and Suffering of the Other   63
  Stealing the Future of the Other   65
Conclusion   66

PART 2: CREATED FOR COVENANT   69

4. The Moment of Silence   71

  The Constitution as Covenant   72
    The Priority of God   73
    Constitutional Priorities   75
  Religious Observance in the Public Schools   77
  The Religious Liberties Amendment   83
  Conclusion   85

5. On Behalf of the Children   89

  Withholding Medical Treatment on Religious Grounds 93
  The Branch Davidians, Child Abuse,
    and the Government Raid on Mt. Carmel 95
  Advocacy on Behalf of Children   100
  Conclusion   102

6. Building Community Today   105

  Going through Jesus to Get to God   106
  Christian Faith in a Land of Many Faiths   111
  The Fallacy of Mainstream and Margin   114
  Conclusion   118

Notes   124

Preface

Every semester students in my course "Contemporary Religious Thought" choose from a number of topics focused on contemporary religious issues for their paper topics and group projects. Three of the most popular topics among the students include the significance of family values for U.S. politics, the First Amendment right to religious freedom, and the Branch Davidians. I always learn from my students, but some of them merit special gratitude for their fine research. Larry Johnson's work on family values, the papers written by Mike Murray and Sarah Clopton on constitutional issues, and the research done by Paul Whitney and Maxwell Heathcott on the Branch Davidians aided me greatly. I am also grateful to Rev. Lib McGregor-Simmons and the members of the University Presbyterian Church who signed on with me for a Sunday morning class on family values, gender, and religious freedom. Through their very thoughtful engagement, they helped me think through my own theological position. I have written this book largely in response to the concerns voiced by the people whom I have taught and who have taught me, both in the academic classroom and in the church.

Other conversation partners who came to my aid in the process of writing this book include my colleagues Milner Ball, Caldwell Professor of Constitutional Law at the University of Georgia; Doug Brackenridge, Professor of Religion at Trinity University; Linell Cady, Professor of Religion at Arizona State University; Sheila Davaney, Associate Professor of Theology at the Iliff School of Theology; Frank Garcia, Professor of Religion at Trinity University; George Khushf, Assistant Professor of Philosophy at the University of South Carolina; and Richard Niebuhr, Hollis Professor of Divinity at Harvard Divinity School. Margaret Miksch deserves special thanks for proofreading manuscript copy. I thank reference librarians Norma Carmack, Mary Clarkson, and Carl Hanson of the Elizabeth Coates Maddux Library at Trinity University for their assistance in tracking bibliographical resources through Westlaw, Infotrack, and newspaper archives. In addition, I thank Angie Partida for encouraging me to send a proposal for the book to Westminster John Knox Press. Most of all, I owe a very special debt of gratitude to Jon Berquist, my editor, for his prompt and very careful reading, his excellent comments, his confidence in this project, and his strong support every step of the way.

This book represents a family affair. Without my immediate family, as well as my family of origin, I could not have written it. Phil Nichols helped with the bibliographical research and with proofreading the final draft, as well as with his unceasing emotional support. Ben Cooey-Nichols, a very close reader, a demanding critic, and our son, did a stunning job of first-round editing. I dedicate the results of all this energy to my mother, Polly; my sister, Starr; and my brother, Billy—companion survivors who have gone on to thrive—and to the memory of my father, Bill—who conquered his inner demons, only to die too soon for the rest of us.

FAMILY, FREEDOM, AND FAITH

Introduction

The photograph on the facing page comes from my own family album. The occasion is the evening before Easter, April 15, 1995. Most of the members of my family of origin have gathered together to witness the baptism and confirmation of my brother, Billy (upper right), and his two children, Meghan and Heath (foreground), as Catholics. My brother's wife, Kelley (lower right), was confirmed on Pentecost Sunday the year before. In addition to my brother, his wife, and their two children, the subjects in the photograph include my mother, Polly; my sister, Starr, with her husband, David, and their son, Jonathan; my husband, Phil (upper left), and me (center). (Our son, Ben, was unable to make the trip, though when we called him the next day, every family member present talked to him to make sure he felt included in our celebration.) In the photograph we stand with our heads held high, scrubbed and dressed in our best clothes, on the steps of my brother's family's home in Woodstock, Georgia. My brother, Billy, standing at the top of the stairs with his arms outstretched, is presenting us in all our glory to the world and to the neighbor who consented to take the photograph.[1] The event marks a very happy occasion for us all.

Family resemblances notwithstanding, the members of this family differ greatly in certain significant ways. We work very different jobs, hold to different philosophies of child rearing, vote different politics, and confess different faiths. Our vocations include teaching, warehouse supervising, administrative services, mortgage lending, landscaping, and working in the home. Though all of us unquestionably love our children and seek to foster their best interests, we have disciplined them differently and taught them values that reflect our political and religious differences. Much to my mother's wonder, my brother, my sister, and I each voted for different presidential candidates in the 1992 election. My mother was brought up within the Disciples of Christ, and my father, now dead, was reared Southern Baptist. My sister and her family are Methodist and my own family is Presbyterian. Although from Catholic to Baptist, all of the confessions are Christian, the religious differences among us, along with our political and philosophical differences, have provoked much dispute in the past. Nevertheless, on this occasion we have mellowed; we wish simply to share the joy of the new life found by my brother and his family.

While there have been many such occasions of joy in this family, including marriages, births, christenings, baptisms, graduations, and vocational successes, this photograph, and the many others like it, tell only part of the story. Not one adult among the subjects of this particular photograph has avoided pain. Only two of the adults standing on those steps have escaped suffering at the hands of members of their own families of origin. We not only number among the walking wounded, some of us have inflicted some of the damage, albeit unintentional at the time. Our private stories, as opposed to our public faces, are sometimes stories of near defeat, temporary defeat, and finally the small triumphs that build slowly into survival and partial healing. That my brother, my sister, and I went on to help form families of our own is first and foremost a tribute to an unconventional, nonnuclear family. The credit goes to my mother's courageous efforts as a single parent, the support of my godmother and our maternal grandparents, and the patience of the people with whom we later made new lives. It could have been different.

This book is about the religious and political diversity human beings bring to the public arena. It is about the private stories of domestic violence as well. The connecting point is family values. The family in which I grew up is not particularly unusual, either in its religious and political diversity or in the afflictions its members have suffered. Private stories of abuse within the family are appallingly ordinary. In over sixteen years of teaching undergraduate students I have listened to countless stories of domestic battering and sexual abuse from my students representing highly diverse political, religious, and economic backgrounds. I have taught victims of incest and students whose religiously conservative parents beat them for coming out as homosexuals, students who were regularly beaten as children by alcoholic fathers and students who feared for their mothers' safety in the home, students whose families lost their homes due to sudden unemployment and students whose highly affluent parents emotionally and spiritually abandoned them at a very early age.

My research confirms what my experience all too often presents to me. There is every cause for alarm at what is happening within families and to them in this country. Indeed, there was cause for alarm long before the concept *family values* entered public discourse. On the one hand, domestic violence makes the U.S. home one of the most dangerous places in the world for adult women and for children and the elderly of both genders to live. On the other hand, violence in the streets, focused largely on young adult males, destroys families as well. Although poverty plays no small role in both domestic and street violence, poverty alone does not account for all of it. For example, domestic violence does not respect class distinctions; one need not be poor to be its victim. Furthermore, poverty itself results from violence done by the institutions of global and state capitalism in concert with the neglect and deterioration of a sense of a public or common good on the part of our citizenry. Personal responsibility plays a role as well—not only the personal responsibility of the individual perpetrators of violence, but of those who do little or nothing to stop violence, namely, elected politicians and voters themselves.

What is happening to families should obviously be at the top of the list of national concerns in a democracy, for healthy democracy depends on the well-being of its citizenry and the well-being of citizens depends on the well-being of the families who nourish them. Nevertheless, it should also be kept in mind that the role of the state in family life is ambiguous. Government in this country, at every level, has on more than one occasion sought to regulate family life in oppressive and authoritarian ways; at the same time, government has also often neglected and abandoned its poorest and most helpless citizens. We should never lose sight of the limitations of government when discussing the plight of families.

Deterioration of family life should be at the top of the list of spiritual and theological concerns as well, for reasons that may not be so obvious in a secular country. Religion has played a double role in family life. Religious institutions have not only played a role in the liberation of some people, they have also historically sought to regulate families, sometimes in highly coercive ways. So, for example, parents have justified on religious grounds battering their children as a form of discipline. They have denied their own adolescent children access to information on reproduction, birth control, and abortion and have sometimes made this same information difficult to obtain in the public arena for children whose parents do not share their beliefs. In this country the constitutional guarantee of separation of religion and state works against religious coercion; nevertheless, even this constitutional right is at risk today.

This threat to freedom from religious coercion by the state requires a theological response as well as a political one. Many Christians are presently involved in challenging the separation of religion and state. The justifications they give for their actions are often theological. Well-meaning people, seeking to be true to their deepest spiritual convictions, actively support the legislation of religious regulation of family life, in the name of family values. They have organized very effective lobbying groups, chief among them the Christian Coalition, in order to effect a very specific agenda on family values. This agenda includes proposals for legislation that, if enacted, would seriously erode the First Amendment, the rights of parents to bring up their children differently from what the Coalition views to be normative, and the rights of children to safety in the home. This demand for regulation of religious and family life furthermore does not take into consideration respect for preserving precious and real differences among diverse kinds of families and among the values they embody. If we who value diversity as a conviction of faith do not speak out against such regulation, we have betrayed the very faiths that sustain us.

What and whom are we valuing when we talk about family values? What constitutes a family? What do Christians owe their families and the families of others according to scripture and church teaching? Does scripture provide us with a blueprint for the ideal family? What are the implications of the way we think about family for how we think about the differences between men and women and the freedom we accord them as such? What is the significance of identifying family values with specific forms of Christian faith for Christians who do not agree? Or for people of different religious and political faiths? What role should family values play in shaping our political decisions? In other words, to what kinds of lives does God call us as members of families who are citizens of a secular, religiously plural, democratic republic?

The last three national elections, as well as recent state and local elections, have focused increasingly on family values. Both political parties use a rhetoric that connects family values to religious concerns and symbols. This practice continues into the present. In spring 1995 during the national memorial service mourning casualties of the bombing of the Alfred P. Murrah Federal Building in Oklahoma City, President Bill Clinton spoke of "a terrible sin" that "took the lives of some of our American family."[2] Shortly thereafter, the Republican congressional leadership unveiled the *Contract with the American Family*, a ten-point program for future national legislation, designed by the Christian Coalition.

Both Clinton's view and the view of the Republican-supported Christian Coalition clearly connect family to a sense of identity that is at once religious and national, though the respective identities differ starkly from each other. On the one hand, Republicans and conservative Democrats from the religious right have emphasized what they view to be a divinely ordained, nuclear family, headed by a father as the primary, if not sole, breadwinner, and ultimate authority. Moderate and liberal Democrats, on the other hand, have emphasized a "new covenant" between the nation as all-inclusive family and each individual American family, regardless of the form the family unit takes. What difference does it make which view prevails? Are there other, better models for how family and civic life are related, and need they necessarily be religious? What role, if any, should family values, however they are defined, play in making political choices?

This book analyzes, from a Reformed Protestant theological perspective, current political and religious conflict surrounding the concept *family values*. It explores conflicting views of what family means and the political and theological implications of these values for religious and political freedom. In regard to human freedom, it focuses specifically on the significance of family values for conceiving gender difference and for interpreting the First Amendment guarantee of freedom of religion. Having explored the conflicting views of family and the values associated with them in regard to gender and constitutional issues, I propose a constructive theological position that supports concern for family life in the context of secularity, religious and political diversity, and social justice. I hope to provide a theological framework for Christians concerned with family issues, who also value secularity, diversity, and social justice, to begin to think through their own responses in regard to public policy and political decision making.

I represent a position that is critical of both liberalism and conservatism as we presently know them, though I propose a constructive alternative as well. Extremists of the religious right, most notably the Christian Coalition, with the support of many conservative Republicans and Democrats in Congress, claim to be fostering family values while seeking to balance the federal budget, reduce the federal debt, and deregulate federal government. Their discourse is a rhetoric of "getting government off our backs." Nevertheless, the legislation presently pending under their watch cuts urgently needed relief to indigent families, while intruding into individual privacy and family life in ways damaging to both individuals and families alike. Though claiming only to promote religious freedom and parental rights, the Christian Coalition in particular would infringe on First Amendment freedoms and the rights of parents and children who do not share the particular values of the Coalition.

By the same token, religious liberals simply have not addressed family life as such; liberals have instead tended to think in terms of advocacy of particular groups of oppressed people without reference to specific concerns for family and with insufficient reference to the significance of gender, race, age, and class for understanding the difficulties families presently face. Furthermore, political liberals have tended to assume that concerns for family life can be adequately addressed by focusing on individual rights and on large programs that administer aid to indigent families without input from these families regarding their actual needs. As a result, indigent families suffer social stigma, needless entanglement with bureaucracy, and inadequate treatment of their problems.

Whereas the politicized religious right has tended to advocate on behalf of parents without consideration of the rights of children in ways potentially and actually detrimental to children, its counterparts on the left have advocated for children, sometimes in ways detrimental to them and to their parents. The alternatives I propose to these failures emphasize the decision-making processes that determine family life and self-government, as well as specific programs in themselves.

The book is divided into two parts according to theological themes. Part 1, "Created in the Image of God," which includes the first three chapters, focuses on the meaning of the theological claim, based on Genesis 1:26–27, that we are created in the image of God. These chapters focus on the significance of this claim for defining the concept *family*. Community today, as in the past, depends on a willingness to commit to the covenants we make with God and with one another. Part 2, "Created for Covenant," which includes the last three chapters, explores the significance of the image of God in respect to the covenants God has established with some of the people of God. The chapters in this section connect *covenant* to *constitution* and address the issue of what *family* means for Christians in a secular, religiously plural society established by constitutional law.

In Part 1, chapter 1 explores the concept *family*. In order to establish a context for thinking critically about family values, it examines representations of family life in the Christian Bible and in American literature. These texts hold in common a myriad of troubling images of family life. They also share a historic concern to redeem families from the external circumstances that threaten their well-being, as well as from their own worst impulses toward self-destruction. As authoritative texts they have served as resources for Christians concerned with family life in a variety of different ways.

The biblical texts in particular are subject to conflicting interpretations. Chapter 2 addresses some of these conflicts. Nowhere are these conflicts more stark than in two books recently published by evangelical Protestants Ralph Reed and Jim Wallis. Both thinkers depend heavily on appropriation of biblical texts; yet, where they focus and how they interpret lie 180 degrees apart. Their very different positions merit special attention, for they virtually set the limits of current public discussion, within Christian, especially Protestant, circles of the relation between faith and politics as centered by concerns for family.

Reed, author of *Politically Incorrect* and executive director of the Christian Coalition, of which Pat Robertson is president, serves as chief architect of the *Contract with the American Family*.[3] Wallis, author of *The Soul of Politics* and representative of the evangelical left as a founder of Sojourners, issued, along with ninety other church leaders, the *Cry for Renewal* as a counterresponse to the *Contract with the American Family*.[4] *Politically Incorrect*, a defense of the agenda of the Christian Coalition, presents Reed's vision for America. It idealizes male-headed, nuclear families as divinely ordained. Taken in conjunction with the *Contract with the American Family*, it constitutes a blueprint for establishing such families as normative for this country. Reed refers to the constituency he represents as "the people of faith," whom he identifies as religious conservatives whose values are in fact mainstream values. By contrast, Wallis seeks to represent "the People of God," whom he understands to include everyone by virtue of the creation of all human beings in the image of God. He and others who share his commitment to social justice stress a Christian commitment to a politics that rejects both conservatism and liberalism as currently practiced. This politics of social justice commits instead to empowering the dispossessed, irrespective of their family configurations and their religious or nonreligious alignments. What is the theological and political significance of this difference in constituencies to which these two leaders hold themselves accountable? What are the implications of this difference for how we think about family life?

Chapter 3 discusses the significance of difference by looking at how we interpret gender difference in light of the Genesis account of the creation of Adam and Eve. It focuses primarily on the interaction of family and faith in terms of what it means to be men and women. How one views the family in relation to faith reflects and shapes how one understands sexual or gender difference. The way one understands difference in relation to power affects who gets to decide how families are configured and what freedoms are available to family members. The significance we attribute to difference, whether in regard to gender, race, ethnicity, class, or age, often has devastating economic implications for underemployed and unemployed young adult males, female-headed, single-parent families, abused children, and the elderly. An extended analysis of the limitations of how we think about difference in relation to violence makes this devastation abundantly clear.

Just as the way we value families shapes and reflects the freedom we accord men as men and women as women, our family values likewise shape and reflect how we interpret and act upon our constitutionally guaranteed freedom of religion. Whenever family values represent the values of a particular religious community elevated to absolute status as binding on all citizens, negative consequences follow for the exercise of traditional constitutional rights by citizens of this country, particularly the exercise of freedom of religion.

In Part 2, chapters 4 and 5 address at length relations between the family and the state in the context of religious rights and responsibilities. After a brief overview of the history of the Supreme Court's various positions on First Amendment guarantees of religious freedom, I analyze two areas of conflict over religious freedom: the Court's decisions on religious observance in the schools and the problems entailed in the state's intervention into family life in religious contexts on behalf of the welfare of children. Examples of contexts in which the state has intervened include families who, on religious grounds, refuse conventional medical treatment for their minor children and Attorney General Janet Reno's justification for the raid by federal agents on the Branch Davidians at Mt. Carmel in Waco, Texas, on the grounds of child abuse.

I conclude Part 2 by offering a positive theological alternative to what I consider to be the excesses of the religious right, the neglect of crucial family issues by the religious left, and the neglect and failures of both political parties. Chapter 6 articulates a theological framework that provides an alternative to the identification of religion and state through family values that occurs on both sides of the political fence. It explores Jesus' ambivalence toward families, the church's historic assumption and extension of the role of family, and the present place of the church as a member of a wider earth household.

People who expect either simple, absolute definitions or extended philosophical discussions of the concepts *family, freedom,* and *faith* need read no farther. Apart from confessing that the God who requires justice (Micah 6:8) is the origin of all three, I argue for finding ways to sustain multiple meanings for these concepts. In recognition that faith comprehends practice as well as attitude, I make concrete, sometimes very specific suggestions all the way through this discussion for Christians to explore together and to implement within our confessing communities and beyond them in our civic life. From rethinking the role of godparents to inventing the role of godchildren, to placing personal computers into the laps of poor people, the one consistent theme throughout is the need to find those avenues that empower more and more people, regardless of their religious faith or lack of it, to take charge of and to contribute responsibly to the communal processes that govern their lives. After all, this is how democracy works and what community should be all about.

Part 1

Created in the Image of God

1

Images of the Family

During the 1992 Republican national convention, Patrick Buchanan declared war on what he viewed to be the political, moral, and spiritual excesses of the political left. By "political left" he meant secular liberals and moderates, feminists, homosexuals, academics who question moral absolutism and argue for cultural diversity, artists whose art challenges conventional sexual norms and their supporters, and those who represent the media industries, just to name a few of the opponents. At the time Buchanan, formerly a presidential candidate himself, sought to represent a movement of politically activist, religiously conservative Christians that has since come to dominate the Republican Party, particularly in the form of the Christian Coalition. Speaking on the movement's behalf, he argued powerfully for a fight to the death between what he viewed to be two diametrically opposed cultures—one religious and pro-family, the other not only secular, but antireligious and anti-family—a fight in which the pro-family movement he represented would ultimately triumph. For Buchanan, that Christians would be feminist, lesbian, gay, academic, artistic, or affiliated with communications media, and that these Christians might advocate on behalf of families, appears to have fallen outside the realm of possibility.

There is indeed a war over culture going on, and family life is one of the major battlegrounds. Who the opponents are is far less clear than Buchanan portrays, however. Rather, confusion reigns as people try to figure out what is happening and where they stand in the midst of conflicting views. The struggle ranges from family life to political freedom, to the very meaning of faith itself.

Concerns for family connect directly to human freedom in regard to issues of gender difference and issues of rearing children. The way we think about family shapes and reflects how we think about gender difference, as well as other differences among us. Thus, whatever public policy we make, affecting race, class, and gender issues, reflects and informs the extent to which we are willing to practice the universal equality we preach as a representative democracy. Moreover, because family life involves the religious and moral upbringing, education, health care, and disciplining of children, public policy governing family life involves directly and indirectly our constitutionally guaranteed freedom of religion as well.

Concerns for family also relate directly to faith. Because we participate in representative democracy, we have input into the processes that shape public policy through the vote and through political activism informed by the values that reflect our various faiths. The input we contribute reflects the convictions we hold. The present divisions among us emerge not only from profound political differences but from theological differences regarding the meaning of faith itself. Rather than simply a struggle between the secular forces of evil and the religious, predominantly Christian forces for good, the struggle reflects division among Christians and among other religious people as well.

This book seeks to clarify, from a Protestant perspective, what is at stake in the current conflicts over family, the implications of how we think about family life for human freedom, and the sometimes very different theological assumptions from which people who seek to live in faith make the decisions on which they act. Clarification, however, requires pointing out how very complex the issues surrounding family, freedom, and faith really are. Those who would have us believe that there are easy answers to the many social and cultural dilemmas we now face mislead us. In spite of our yearnings to be freed from the difficult religious and political obligations we face as responsible people, we must nevertheless avoid the seductions of oversimplification and narrow self-interest.

Family as Cultural and Political Battleground

Taking responsibility includes first and foremost avoiding the seduction of a trench mentality of "us" versus "them"; we cannot afford to transfer what was once the demonization characteristic of the Cold War now to the home front. Rather, the struggle in which we presently engage amounts to nothing less than a struggle for justice and liberty for all members of all families and for the repair of the earth that sustains their lives. All other conflicts we wage take place within this wider struggle in which there ultimately is no "they," only a "we." The struggle over the family occurs within this wider framework. We must not lose sight of this broader context.

This wider framework does not diminish the seriousness of the ongoing conflict over family life presently dominating much of our current public discussion, however. How we determine public policy on family life interacts with all other political determinations; conversely, there is no public policy we make that does not eventually, if not immediately, affect family life. Because of this web of political interactions, because of the specifically religious context in which the public debate on family occurs, and because of the division the debates cause among ourselves, we all the more urgently need to examine the interaction of family, freedom, and faith. This kind of examination requires asking hard questions rather than avoiding them. Since one of the issues at stake here is faith itself, these questions will be theological as well as political in nature. Theological questions notwithstanding, the constitutional prohibition against the establishment of a state religion means that the government of this country must necessarily be secular.

In this country, secularity stands in tension with a civil religion that purports to belong to no specific religious tradition, though it is monotheistic and though it has become a ceremonial and rhetorical tradition in its own right. This civil religion involves national religious observances on public occasions. Thus the pledge of allegiance pledges loyalty to one nation "under God"; elected officials take office by swearing on the Christian Bible to uphold the Constitution; legal tender is engraved with the motto "In God we trust"; our legislative bodies open their sessions with prayer; and elected officials continually invoke the name of God in their speeches. The courts have ruled that, because government endorses no specific historical religious tradition or institution when observing these practices, such observances do not establish a state religion.[1] Christians thus practice their faith in this country in a social context that mixes secularity with religious observances that vaguely resemble some of the practices of Christian faith, but are not identical with them.

This mix, or some would say confusion, of religious practices with secularity in a religiously diverse country means, among other things, that Christian views of family will involve necessarily some consideration of secular views of family, even if by way of rejecting them on religious grounds as inappropriate for some Christians. It also means that from time to time some Christians may seek to conform American civil religious practices more closely to Christian traditions, thereby creating serious problems for people of other faiths, including nonreligious, secular faiths.[2]

Religious faith practiced in relatively secular context inevitably produces conflicts, particularly with respect to what qualifies as desirable family life.

For example, it is one thing to act politically out of the religious conviction that, by virtue of God's having created humans in the image of God, all humans are sisters and brothers. It is an altogether different matter to attempt to legislate, out of religious conviction, that all families must conform to certain patterns or structures and that they must practice certain values in order to receive certain government-mandated benefits. The first case constitutes individual action; the second case constitutes government intervention on religious grounds and is, in its effects, the establishment of a state religion.

Christians have historically sought political reform in both ways, and we still continue to do so, thus generating conflict among ourselves. Indeed, Christians are acting in both ways as many of us find ourselves engaged in lively legal and political disputes with one another over the significance and quality of family life. These disputes occur in a context that is both religious and political; they also have a history that precedes and informs them. In addition to political discourse, the rhetoric used is often a theological rhetoric, one that on occasion more than flirts with idolatry by treating partial and finite religious and moral values as if they were universal and absolute. In addition to theological underpinnings, these disputes have serious implications for the civil liberties of all citizens in this country, whether directly involved in current debates or not, whether identified as religious or secular, and whether identified primarily in terms of family membership, some other affiliation, or simply as individual persons.

These disputes depend on assumptions about what *family* means, what family values are, and who gets to decide public policy—assumptions that we often do not explore, by virtue of their being assumptions. What we are willing to accept as a normative shape, configuration, or pattern of family structure and what we consider to be the determining characteristics of family life lie at the heart of current controversies surrounding family values. The purpose of this chapter and the next is to explore some of these assumptions by raising a series of questions: What counts as a family? What do family values value? Who gets to decide? What counts as family is precisely the point of contention over which various religious and secular groups currently struggle.

What Counts as Family?

It would be comforting to think that we can define *family* in simple terms and that the meaning is given entirely by God and nature, and therefore not dependent on what we think or do. Simple definitions would relieve us of the enormous burden of contributing to the meaning we seek to find. Indeed, this view that the meaning of *family* is already given in such a manner prevails among the activists of the Christian right and serves as the central point of contention in disputes surrounding family values. Nevertheless, family is one of those realities the meaning for which humans bear responsibility in both conscious and unconscious ways. The concept *family* rests to some degree on biological grounds and, from a perspective of Christian faith, to some extent on theological grounds. Family is nevertheless one of those realities that not only shapes humans, but is also shaped by humans through the laws they make, the religious observances they practice, and the theories and theologies they construct. The social meaning of the concept *family* has a history that has shifted over time. This history is until recently a predominantly religious history. An analysis of the interaction of the biological and social meaning of *family* with special attention to its religious context illustrates just how difficult it is to determine what counts as family today.

No matter how we grew up, no matter how much we differ from one another, no matter what our religious or secular convictions, all human beings are somebody's children. In this narrow, biological sense we are each and every one of us members of some family. In a broader biological sense, by virtue of being human, we are all members of the same "kind," or kin to one another. Kinship as members of humankind and family membership in its narrower sense are givens, for better or for worse. We do not choose to join the human family. Likewise, though mates may choose each other and may choose to have or not to have children, as parents they do not choose the specific children they get. Children similarly do not pick their parents under biological circumstances. Biology alone, nevertheless, does not define the meaning of *family*.

Biological definitions of parentage and birth barely begin to define what we mean in this culture when we talk about family. People may choose to reproduce biologically in ways that involve a donor who is technically "outside" the immediate family, someone who will play no role whatsoever in parenting any offspring from the relationship; the donor's donation may result from any number of possible social arrangements ranging from technological agreements to casual sexual liaisons. Furthermore, people may become parents through adopting children rather than through procreation. Thus, in addition to biology, there is a social element as well.

Marriage itself is a social arrangement, often authorized and validated on religious grounds. Marriage in Western culture emerges originally as an economic transaction arranged by the parents of the bride and the bridegroom. In some cultures the male was expected to take more than one wife, as well as concubines. Furthermore, wives were themselves the legal property of their husbands, and divorce was taboo. Today we in effect practice serial polygamy. Marriages frequently end and remarriages occur in ways that reshape family patterns by expanding the biological and social relations among children resulting from the multiple relations of their parents. Moreover, marriage and reproduction no longer necessarily imply each other. Adults who have no intention of reproducing and rearing children form permanent lasting relations that endure from relative youth to old age and death, and people who reproduce do not necessarily marry.

As if things were not complicated enough already, we also use the term *family* as a metaphor for all kinds of other meaningful religious, political, social, and economic relations and communities to which we choose to commit. In short we can say that families are sociobiological arrangements that are in some respects, but not entirely, chosen—arrangements often made on religious grounds. To have said this much, however, is still to have hardly said anything at all. For example, we have in no way addressed the role family life plays in shaping the social and individual identities of persons, nor have we acknowledged that in so doing, families, whether so-called healthy or dysfunctional, bring out the very best and the very worst in each of us.

As members of families we grow up embedded in a web of interactions ranging from nurture to neglect and abuse. These interactions play a central, though not exclusive, role in determining who we are as persons throughout our entire lives. They depend on circumstances and conditions over which parents or the adults in charge have little or no control, including economic and social interactions, as well as personal psychological histories. These interactions depend on personal responsibility or irresponsibility as well. This mix of conditions over which children within families have no control and the adults in charge have only partial control forces on us questions of distinguishing among and responding to individual, communal, and national responsibilities for sustaining as good a quality of life for each and every family member as possible. The issues of responsibility and accountability inform much of the discussion now occurring in a religious context.

Families as we know them today are thus relatively new to human history. The history of the development of family patterns into their present forms is long and complex. Suffice it to say that highly mobile, small, nuclear families emerging from romantic liaisons between consenting heterosexual adults appear very late on the historical scene. Uncontested divorce in which the custody of children is shared and the property held by adults is divided equally is even more recent. In this country, until the twentieth century, wives and children remained the property of husbands and fathers; women were denied the right to vote; and for the most part divorce was unheard of. As recently as two decades ago marital rape was still considered a contradiction in terms; furthermore, the concept is still subject to legal and theological contention. Last but not least, business corporations increasingly recognize long-term, same-sex partnerships as constituting relationships due the same legal rights and benefits as heterosexual marriages. The meaning of the concept *family* has not only dramatically changed over time, but will continue to change in the face of economic and political pressure.

Biblical Images of the Family

When we turn from biological, sociological, and psychological accounts of family life to Jewish and Christian scriptures and the practices and stories they record, we find that, depending on the lens through which we view these sources, they will paint very different pictures of family life. Much of the rhetoric on family values coming from some religious conservatives draws on specific, debatable interpretations of select texts from Jewish and Christian scriptures, which they view through the lens of nostalgic idealizations of family life from an ostensible American past, located sometimes in the nineteenth century and sometimes in the 1950s. Shrouded in a nostalgia for a past that arguably never existed, these texts and images serve as authoritative blueprints for family life, to be implemented through legislation at local, state, and national levels. By contrast, religious liberals, at least liberal Christian theologians, have tended simply to ignore the implications of scriptural narrative for family life as such, although particularly during the Christmas season, liberals, like their conservative counterparts, tend to sentimentalize the birth of Jesus.

Since we all view scripture through the lens of our values regardless of which period of time we draw them from, it is important to look at alternative biblical and biblically influenced literary representations of the family and compare these with the blueprints presented by the religious right to the public as authoritative. The narratives of biblical figures like Ishmael, Hagar, Tamar, Job, Ruth, and Naomi, among many others, stand in striking contrast to the picture painted by political activists of the religious right, for these narratives paint grim and complex pictures of family life, though not entirely humorless and without hope. Focusing on these narratives allows us to realize that the sufferings within families, their struggles, and the concern to heal and reconcile them are not new. Rather, suffering, struggle, and concern are all as old as attempts to

regulate family life through historically conditioned codes and the nostalgia for an ideal family that never was, or was at best typical of a very
few families. This does not mean that the plight of today's families and
concern for that plight is trivial, but it does mean that codes taken out of
historical context and the nostalgia that accompanies them provide little
or no solution to the problems that beset family life. The difference in se-
lections of biblical resources exemplifies one more instance of the present
cultural struggle to determine the direction in which society or culture
will proceed.

The family that those on the religious right represented by the Christian Coalition seek to promote and to protect is first and foremost a male-
dominated, heterosexual nuclear family with children. The male is ordained by God according to scripture, specifically the Genesis story of
Adam and Eve, the maleness of Christ as head of the church, and the
household codes of the New Testament, to head the household. "Head
of household" means in this context that the husband has ultimate authority over the family, though the wife may have full responsibility for
specifically domestic matters, as well as shared economic responsibility
for keeping the family going. This pattern alone serves as the ethically
and religiously normative blueprint for family life.

While women may work outside the home, should economic necessity require it, their primary role is that of helper, understood as subor-
dinate who bears primary responsibility, though not authority, to support
and promote the well-being of the family in the domestic realm. This role
of helpmeet plays itself out chiefly in fulfilling the duties of wife and
mother, both of which are often highly romanticized in terms of sexual
purity in images borrowed from stereotypic middle-class families of either the Victorian era or the 1950s. I say "stereotypic" because historians
and social analysts of both periods argue that the representations of men,
women, and family to which the leaders of the religious right appeal either never existed or were not typical of their times.[3] Any children resulting from this union are brought up to be God-fearing, obedient both
to God and to civil authorities, sexually chaste, and loyal to their country, like their parents. They are furthermore brought up according to
stereotyped conceptions of gender difference so that they may fulfill their
proper, God-ordained, gender-defined roles as adults. Within this family pattern religious faith and practices connect with a political activism
that assumes and promotes identifying the will of the father, the national
will, and the will of God with each other. According to this theological
identification, the will of God is in theory authoritative even over father
and country. In practice, God's will usually gets identified with the fa-

ther's interest in preserving domination and with the national self-interest according to a politically conservative perspective.[4]

This kind of conservative appeal to scripture notwithstanding, the Hebrew and Christian Bibles actually present us with much more complex pictures of family life. These pictures on occasion even conflict. They emerge both from a variety of codes regulating family life and from narratives or stories of the lives of various biblical figures.

As some representatives of the pro-family movement are quick to point out, numerous codes regulate how families should be organized, regulate sexual practices, and define religious practices along gender lines. The codes range from the Ten Commandments and the Levitical codes in the Hebrew Bible and the Christian Old Testament to the codes governing the life of the early Christian communities in the New Testament. In the Hebrew Bible and the Christian Old Testament these codes govern everything from adultery, extramarital lust, menstruation, and dispersal of semen to the length of women's hair (see, for example, Leviticus 12:2, 5 and Genesis 34:14–15). Continuing in a similar vein, New Testament codes recommend to men and women that it is better to marry than to lust; in addition they exhort women to obey their husbands, not to speak in church, and to cover their heads during worship (see, for example, 1 Corinthians 7:1–39 and Ephesians 5).

The codes themselves have generated much scholarly and theological controversy.[5] To what extent are they even translated correctly? When properly translated, how are they to be interpreted? In light of God's expulsion of the first couple from Eden (Genesis 3:22–24), in light of the new covenant written on the heart according to the prophet Jeremiah (Jeremiah 31:31), or in light of the reconciliation promised in Galatians 3:28? If they are not to be taken literally, are these codes binding in any respect? If so, how do we determine which codes are binding and who gets to decide?

Jews and Christians alike struggle with these issues as they arise in relation to their own historical situations. In my opinion, with the exceptions of the commandments against adultery and covetousness, the codes are no more binding than the codes governing master-slave relations that often accompany them. As such they reflect the limitations of the cultures out of which they arise. The commandments against adultery and coveting are exceptions by virtue of being among the Ten Commandments, which have enjoyed a theologically privileged status as the centerpiece of Torah or the Law. But even the commandments against adultery and covetousness are subject to interpretation and modification, not unlike the prohibition against killing. Just as theologians have been willing to make exceptions in regard to self-defense and in times of war, so theologians have reinterpreted the two commandments regulating marriage. For example, the prohibition against covetousness, taken literally, is binding only on men and assumes that wives, like houses, maidservants, manservants, oxen, and asses are property. Instead of taking the commandment literally, many theologians have reinterpreted the commandment to be binding on men and women alike and often ignored the obvious identification of wives as property and the references to slaveholding.

In other words, such codes, including the Ten Commandments, when taken out of their own cultural context, in some cases mistranslated, and oftentimes interpreted literally as moral absolutes, have little if any authority as blueprints for the present. They nevertheless perform important functions as reminders and as records of attempts to make covenant relations to establish justice.

As reminders they demonstrate that communities and societies require some kind of governance in order to form themselves. Such codes furthermore address the historical situations in which the communities and societies find themselves. As such they often represent the interests and values of those who have the power to make them. They therefore hold important theological significance, for they remind us that no expression of faith escapes the culture in which it appears, and no culture escapes the human sinfulness of abusing power. Furthermore, they remind us that religion is oppressive and authoritarian as well as spiritually nourishing. The codes are likewise theologically interesting because they sometimes contrast in important ways with what I understand to be Jesus' ambivalence toward families, a subject for later discussion. The New Testament codes in particular are of historical interest because they seem to assume a family pattern more closely akin to a nuclear family than the earlier codes, though not entirely identical with what we understand to be nuclear families today. They thus serve as historical data in understanding how family patterns develop over time.

In addition to serving as reminders, some of these codes, most notably Torah itself, represent covenants. As covenants, their partiality and corruption notwithstanding, they exemplify God's *way* of redeeming humans, repairing injustice, and making real God's sovereignty on earth in spite of human sin. The process of covenant making by which God redeems humans should be distinguished, however, from the very human codes that result.

In short, the biblical codes regulating family life are to some extent necessary, nevertheless highly variable, often corrupt testimonies to a human need for redemption and for community, as well as to a community's failure to meet this need. We cannot live without some pattern to social life in order to establish responsibility for child rearing and the care of the elderly, but most family patterns, when taken as absolute, often wreak havoc on the lives of the people they are supposed to protect and nourish.

The biblical narratives depicting family life bear witness to this havoc in great detail. In contrast to the attempts underlying the codes to create and preserve context-specific, usually male-dominated styles or forms of family life as normative, the narratives of God at work in the lives of biblical figures present highly variegated views of family life as well as of God. From the stories of the first family of Adam, Eve, Cain, and Abel, to Jesus' responses to his own family, the stories are stories of conflict, suffering, and survival, sometimes coupled with prophetic concern for justice, mercy, and reconciliation. These stories narrate what happens when the rules either do not work, cannot work, or get broken.

The "first" family of Genesis confronts the entry of sin into the world, followed by Cain's act of fratricide. The "last" family of the Gospels struggles with the possibility of unwed motherhood, the near murder of Jesus in his infancy at the hands of the state, and his brutal, ignominious death as a criminal convicted by the state. In between these two sets of narrative occurs a multitude of stories of nomads, kings, servants, prophets, priests, sons, daughters, in-laws, cousins, uncles, aunts, husbands, wives, fathers, and mothers whose lives are riven by violence and betrayal, ranging from murder, rape, incest, and adultery to fraud, swindling, disease, and pestilence. This pattern of familial strife producing disaster, in which government and religious officials intervene only to make things worse, is no less characteristic of the New Testament than of the Hebrew Bible and the Christian Old Testament. Consider, for example, the beheading of John the Baptist, as instigated by a mother through her dancing daughter and ordered by a king (Matthew 14:1–12).

These stories, taken together and scrutinized for what they reveal about family life, are significant precisely because they are stories rather than blueprints. They are stories that may end happily, but more often end ambiguously. When taken at face value rather than sanitized by ecclesiastical authorities, they are sometimes humorous, sometimes heroic, and almost always violent. They raise deeply troubling questions about suffering, about God, and about what it means to be human, and they are notorious for not providing any easy answers.

For example, what about Hagar and Ishmael, driven from their home by Sarah so that Isaac might count as the firstborn son (Genesis 21:9–21)? Though Hagar and Ishmael survive their flight from Abraham and Sarah and go to Paran, Ishmael has lost his father, and Isaac has lost his half-brother. Moreover, Hagar has lost her protection and security in a male-dominated society. Or consider Tamar, the daughter of David. Whatever happens to Tamar after she is raped by her brother Amnon and flees to her brother Absalom (2 Samuel 13:1–21)? Why does she just drop out of the picture except as the occasion for conflict among her male relatives? Likewise, consider the ending of Job. What kind of compensation is it for God to give Job twice as much as he had before, if what Job lost included his children (Job 42:10)? What kind of justice is at work for the children who lost their lives as a result of a wager between God and Satan?

These tales of family members suffering at the hands of one another, not to mention sometimes at the hands of God, raise nasty theological questions, haunt the heart, and leave loose strings everywhere. They push a reader beyond the available texts, which in themselves stand as absurdities in the face of a quest for meaning. Apart from any context of faith, which in itself will also not provide resolution so much as a way of surviving and trusting in spite of what meets the eye, these stories are devastating. Just like many of the stories many of us could tell of our own family lives, their chief value lies in bearing witness, in giving voice to pain and violation, no matter how absurd, with the hope of moving on to new life, though sometimes this hope remains unfulfilled.

Literary Images of the Family

This tradition of bearing witness to suffering and violence, particularly within the context of family relations, continues into the present in the form of literary fiction that draws upon these biblical and religious themes and images. In the United States this tradition is marked by the work of Nathaniel Hawthorne, Harriet Beecher Stowe, Mark Twain, Willa Cather, Zora Neale Hurston, William Faulkner, Robert Penn Warren, James Baldwin, and Flannery O'Connor among others. In our own times this tradition numbers among its ranks the novels and short stories of John Irving, Paule Marshall, Toni Morrison, Gloria Naylor, Joyce Carol Oates, Jane Smiley, John Updike, and Alice Walker, just to name a few. The stories these authors tell, like the biblical stories that inform them, reveal our values and reflect us back to ourselves in prophetic and humbling ways. Though the stories are works of fiction, they realistically portray the realities of family life in this culture in striking contrast to the images of family portrayed by the religious right.

Three stories are particularly relevant to understanding what constitutes a family as it pertains to current discussions of family values. One story focuses primarily on adultery, one on incest, and the last on slavery and liberation. All three retell earlier stories from a new and different perspective. All three address the issue of violence as characteristic of family life. The first is *Roger's Version* by John Updike; the second, *A Thousand Acres* by Jane Smiley; the third, *Beloved* by Toni Morrison.

In *Roger's Version*, Updike retells Hawthorne's *The Scarlet Letter*, now recast in the late twentieth century and told from the perspective of the cuckold.[6] A tale of an adultery that produces a child, *The Scarlet Letter* represents Hawthorne's critique of what he views to be Puritan sexual repression and hypocrisy. The novel focuses primarily on Hester Prynne, the adulteress. Hawthorne concludes *The Scarlet Letter* by prophesying a liberation from what he perceived to be the rigidities of a Puritan view of families and the damage done to individual family members by Puritan moral absolutes. Hawthorne further connects the story of Hester Prynne to a somewhat optimistic view of the national destiny, which is linked to individual freedom.

By contrast Updike connects his tale of adultery to this country's failure to live up to its promise to its children. In contrast to Hawthorne's narration from the perspective of a relatively detached, omniscient chronicler, Updike's narrator Roger is an Anglo-American, Protestant, Harvard Divinity School professor and ordained minister who is only an ostensible cuckold—ostensible, for we get just one very brief, possible outside confirmation that Roger's wife is actually an adulteress, all her betrayals otherwise taking place as Roger's fantasies. Roger's fantasies of his wife's adultery become a sort of obscene justification for his own adulterous and incestuous relationship with his niece, an adolescent, single, welfare mother of a biracial child.

The tale humorously but relentlessly satirizes upper-middle-class, white American intellectuals, particularly religious sophisticates, in all their self-deception, political hypocrisy, and moral and spiritual bankruptcy. Irony and humor notwithstanding, it is also a poignant tale of the toll that family life in this context takes on its young, both in terms of neglecting them and in terms of physically and sexually abusing them. Like the prophet Hosea before him (Hosea 1:2–8), Updike connects adultery symbolically to a wider social and cultural betrayal, in this case a betrayal of a nation's young by the adults in charge, particularly the males. Adultery further connects theologically both to the idolatry of seeking to prove God's existence with certainty and to the heresy of sinning deliberately and excessively in order that grace may all the more abound. *Roger's Version* serves as a scathing critique of individual, familial, communal, and national failure to protect and to nurture children. Family interactions damage and destroy family members in part due to isolation from wider communities of validation, accountability, and support.

Mobile, urban, nuclear families are particularly vulnerable to this isolation as Updike portrays them.

The isolation of families from wider communities of validation, accountability, and support becomes no less damaging to individual family
members in the context of rural life as portrayed by Jane Smiley in *A
Thousand Acres*. A retelling of *King Lear* from the perspective of one of the
"evil" daughters Goneril, now known as Ginny, *A Thousand Acres* captures rural life for upper-middle-class Anglo-American farm families in
the seventies and eighties in the North American Midwest, a time when
many such families were driven into bankruptcy by overextension of debt.
The stereotype of rural life in this country consists of small communities
whose members are closely bound to one another by religious faith and
by working the land. Images of church socials, Grange Society meetings,
school pageants, everyone pitching in together to build the house or barn,
and everyone pulling together in the midst of adversity are fundamental
to the folklore of American farm life.

Smiley represents an altogether different reality, however. Interne-
cine family struggles between generations over land, the greed of local
bankers all too willing to make bad loans to farmers that result in bank-
rupting them, and the pollution of both land and water by pesticides and
herbicides that produce unusually high rates of cancer and miscarriage
among the farm families form the backdrop for Ginny's struggle to confront sexual abuse by her father. Nostalgic images of farm communities
notwithstanding, it is the victim of incest, not the perpetrator, who bears
its shame in Ginny's story. Church socials turn into occasions of humiliation, and the local pastor simply has no resources for ministering to a
family scarred by sexual and physical violence toward its children.

Isolated by the local community, poisoned by the pollution of the water and the land, abandoned by the church, betrayed by her extramarital
lover, and at odds with every adult member of her immediate family,
Ginny, after a failed attempt to murder her sister Rose, strikes out for a
new life on her own. She re-creates her life in the sober and horrifying
awareness of her own capacity to damage others, as well as her awareness
of the damage done her. Her life is nevertheless the life of a survivor who
later reconciles with the sister she sought to kill, and upon Rose's death
from cancer, Ginny assumes responsibility for raising Rose's daughters.[7]

Like Updike, Smiley illustrates how dependent domestic violence is
on secrecy within the family and denial outside the family. Both authors
portray a horrifying vision of U.S. family life—a life riddled by violence,
emotional abandonment, and isolation from wider communities of accountability and support. Like Updike, Smiley connects this strife to the

failure of economic, political, and religious institutions; however, unlike Updike, Smiley extends her critique of culture to the treatment of the land. We are not only damaging and destroying the families of the present, we are dramatically altering life for future families as well as for other forms of life in destructive and devastating ways.

This awareness that present actions have future implications translates backward into the past as well. For example, U.S. society has yet to take sufficiently into account the extent to which devastation wreaked upon family life in a past slave economy continues to have an impact upon family life for African Americans today. We not only isolate families by structuring them as nuclear families without sufficient communal support, we also abandon them to racism, to sexism, and to poverty.

Toni Morrison's novel *Beloved* captures the devastating consequences of the interaction of sexism and poverty as they are driven by white racism in a slave economy. In an interview Morrison relates how she wrote *Beloved* in response to a newspaper account of a runaway slave woman who killed one of her own children, a clipping bereft of detail and found among archives.[8] Morrison retells this story by imagining what the details might have been in ways that challenge a current, all too racist, but disguised public rhetoric attacking unwed mothers and single-parent welfare mothers. Morrison's fiction in general raises at least two questions relevant to a discussion of family values: What role does racial violence play in the problems that plague African American family life? What role does white racism play in the idealization of the nuclear family?

In answer to the first question *Beloved* presents us with the story of the main character Sethe's struggle to escape slavery, a struggle that is only ironically successful. Having fled through the underground railroad to a free state, Sethe and her children are pursued by her owner and his cohorts. Confronted by their pursuers, and committed to protecting her four children from a life of slavery, she tries to kill the children. She kills one—a baby girl whom she subsequently names Beloved because she has seen "Dearly Beloved" honoring the dead on tombstones. The slave owner refuses to take her back because the killing signifies to him that she is now damaged property, untrustworthy, and therefore useless to him. Thus the killing of Beloved ironically serves to allow the rest of the family to remain in relative freedom. Beloved, however, returns to haunt Sethe in ways detrimental not only to Sethe but to the rest of her family as well. While Sethe finds a relative peace in the end, the plight of Beloved remains unresolved, to be forgotten by later generations. Irony is at work here as well, for though Beloved may be ultimately forgotten by the characters in the novel, we all, black and white, continue to live with the violence of the white racism that produced her and her death.

White people kidnapping black people, bringing them forcibly to this country, treating them as property, breeding them for additional property, selling them without reference to their family configurations, and thus rendering determining kinship lines virtually impossible destroyed family life for the African ancestors of today's African Americans. Though slavery is no longer legal, white racism continues to damage African American life.

In answer to the second question, white racism still disrupts African American family life today. African American family patterns exemplify residual strategies to survive slavery in the past as well as strategies to survive white racism in the present. Toni Morrison reflects some of these strategies for survival not only in *Beloved* but in her other novels as well. She characteristically creates strong networks of female family members who have primary responsibility for preserving their families, who do so exceptionally well, given their circumstances.[9] In *Beloved*, for example, the survival of Sethe and her children depends in part on Sethe's relationship with her mother-in-law, Baby Suggs, a freed slave with whom Sethe sets up housekeeping, in ways that recall the biblical relationship of Ruth and Naomi.

Whereas men play highly valued roles in these women's lives, they do not dominate them, nor are the men in the same position as the women to act to preserve the families themselves, in part but not entirely due to white racism. Racism notwithstanding, many of Morrison's female characters simply do not define themselves centrally in terms of emotional dependence on the men in their lives, though this is not to say that they are incapable of intimacy with men. In *Beloved*, Sethe enters into a relationship with Paul D, also previously a slave belonging to Sethe's owner. Sethe and Paul D share profound intimacy, and Paul D devotes himself to confirming Sethe's worth, which she desperately needs. Nevertheless, as Paul D himself points out in the conclusion, Sethe's worth does not depend on anything external to her, including him or her children, for she is her own "best thing" (Morrison, 273).

These strategies of survival dependent on female networks of support characterize many underclass families today, particularly among African Americans. We need to acknowledge and to respect rather than to devalue these strategies. Instead, public policy makers and conservative religious authorities often impose alien and inappropriate structures as standards by which to measure the eligibility of African American families for Aid for Families with Dependent Children.[10] The media particularly sensationalize minority, unwed, often adolescent mothers on government assistance, and the voting public, sometimes including the black middle class itself, dutifully grows alarmed. These standards and attitudes reflect not only racial and ethnic bias but also sexual bias and prejudice toward the poor.

We fail to note, for example, that families above the poverty level are federally subsidized. The income tax deduction for dependent children, tax credits for day care, deductions for health care, mortgage interest, and property tax, and the property taxes that go to public schools that are paid by citizens who do not have children mean fewer taxes and more income for such families. Furthermore, we accept farm and ranch subsidies, cost overruns in government contracts to private business, and loans to bail out large private corporations as par for the course. This is not to say that entire bureaucratic systems from the Pentagon to Social Security and Welfare do not stand in dire need of reform. Nor am I arguing that families should not receive tax relief in support of the children. But let us be clear about government subsidies. In some form or another almost all of us depend on government subsidies, and the more affluent we are, the greater the benefit. Why then do we focus our zeal for tax reform and deficit cutting on the poor, particularly poor women and their children?

Conclusion

The complexity of actual family patterns as they emerge over time, biblical narrative of family life, and classical and contemporary American fiction raise important questions that are not getting asked in the current discussion and debate surrounding family values. These questions begin with defining what a family is.

What then counts as family? There is no single answer to this question. Actual families include every possible biological, social, and religious configuration of human relations falling within a range of being someone else's child to rearing children of one's own. We are in truth perpetually in the process of defining what *family* means in terms of both the content and the structure of family life, though more intentionally in some historical periods than in others. We are currently involved in intentionally defining *family* right now. Two examples will suffice.

First, the *Contract with the American Family*, designed by the Christian Coalition, calls for tax relief through a $500 tax credit for each child and by individual retirement accounts for mothers in the home, without setting any caps on income. This relief, albeit needed by families with yearly incomes below $50,000, will benefit upper-middle- and upper-income

families as well. Meanwhile Congress is voting massive cuts in government relief for low-income and no-income families. Should Congress enact the legislation necessary to accomplish *both* goals, we will in effect redefine family along class lines. Single-parent female heads of households
with little or no income need not apply.

Second, we are presently engaged in debating whether same-sex cou-
ples constitute families with the same rights as heterosexual families. The
outcome of this particular controversy will determine nothing less than
the rights of homosexual women and men to receive spousal benefits, to
adopt or artificially to bear children, to stand watch at the bedsides of critically ill or dying partners, and to inherit property without challenge from
other family members who are blood kin.

In these cases and others, what counts as family will not be decided
simply by fiat. Rather, the health of the economy and the political, social,
and religious practices that define voting and policy making will determine both the structure of families and the quality of family life. Because
voters vote their convictions, faith has a major role to play here.

As Christians approaching this question, we need to give a critical
primacy to the stories of family life, actual and fictional, that shape and
reflect our past and present. For example, when we turn to what actually
goes on within families and has gone on as long as recorded history, we
find a violence among families that crosses class lines. This recurring violence is not made sufficiently central to discussions of divorce and the
subsequent, so-called broken, home. Instead, all too often public policy
makers and religious leaders assume that two-parent families are by definition good, in contrast to divorced families which are by definition bad.
Not enough people are paying attention to the possibility that divorce,
however tragic, may actually improve a situation, even in the face of economic privation for the mother and children. We normatively define *family* as two parents and their children, and we qualify any variation on this
definition as deviant or aberrant. No one includes in the definition of
family its potential as a location for violence. Nor does anyone include in
the definition of family the problems that arise from poverty, racism, sexism, and heterosexism, themselves conditioned by social violence even
where there is no immediate violence within the home.

Stories of families, actual and fictional, allow us to acknowledge and
to affirm a variety of family configurations as potentially desirable and
normative, rather than seeking a single, ideal blueprint against which to
measure all family patterns. Our criteria for determining desirability
should focus first and foremost on the quality of family life and the well-
being of each individual family member, rather than whether family

structure fits a single, preconceived, blueprint, absolutized for all circumstances. In seeking to make this determination, we need to distinguish the debilitating effects of violence, poverty, and social isolation on
family life, regardless of how families are configured, from the actual configurations themselves. For example, we need to ask whether the problems of single-parent families lie in the fact that they are parented by only
one parent, or in the likelihood that they are economically at risk due to
lack of sufficient child support and adequate day care, as well as to the dep-
rivation of emotional support due to social stigma. Conversely, we need
to acknowledge that two-parent families, simply by virtue of there being
two parents in the household, are not therefore necessarily desirable
places for either the children or the adults to be.

Faith extends beyond consciously held convictions to include un-
consciously made assumptions. More than belief, faith is an attitude
marked by confidence in and loyalty to that which centers it, whether the
center is God, nature, the nation, or the self. This attitude is historically
conditioned by the particular traditions that give it birth and the concrete
practices that nourish it and keep it alive; faith cannot be abstracted from
the history that gives it its particular shape. Nevertheless, faith can point
through its own particularity toward a vision that creates a space that celebrates particularity and difference.[11] The issue in regard to family values is whether faith widens or narrows the possibility of enhancing family life. What kind of faith expands us in response to the members of our
own families and the families of others?[12]

2

Family as
the People of God

No discussion of the interrelations of family, freedom, and faith can occur in a Christian context without reference to God's creation and redemption of human life. According to the Genesis accounts of creation, humans are created in the image of God (Genesis 1:26–28). This image transcends even human sinfulness, a sinfulness from which God redeems humans. According to God's covenants, as exemplified in Torah, in the prophetic traditions, the Gospels, and the epistles, God intends humans for just relations with God, with one another, and with the earth. While the stories of creation and redemption are subject to a variety of different, sometimes conflicting, theological interpretations, they establish, long before the institutional history of Christianity begins, that humans are bound to God, to one another, and to the earth as a family. Thus a discussion of family, freedom, and faith must raise the question of how the family of humankind relates to membership in a particular family.

How Christians relate these stories to their own lives as members of particular families has varied historically in relation to the times in which Christians find themselves and in relation to how particular Christians apprehend scripture to be revelatory. Every generation has had to ask what "family" means and what individual freedom and responsible family membership involve in light of faith. But the limits of these questions are not set by Christian faith alone, nor is the impact of their answers felt only by the Christians who raise the questions. Christian faith finds expression in a number of different ways within Christendom; furthermore, other faiths, notably Jewish and Muslim faiths, share some of the same foundational traditions, though the questions posed and their subsequent responses may differ dramatically. In addition, in this country, monotheistic faith is itself only one possibility among others, secular as well as religious. As U. S. citizens we are dedicated to uphold a form of democracy that, at least in principle, nurtures religious and political diversity. This diversity requires two elements, namely, that no particular religious tradition be established by the state and that people be allowed to express their faith or lack thereof freely.

Whereas the Genesis story establishes from a Christian perspective the human family as the people of God, the people themselves manifest a variety of faiths, including, as is their constitutionally guaranteed right in this country, the belief that there is no God. Just as multiple family structures exist, many and diverse faiths exist. These highly diverse faiths reflect equally diverse systems of valuing family life. That they should come into conflict is hardly surprising. The issue is not so much how to avoid conflict as it is how to resolve it. Will we resolve conflict by insisting that everyone conform to the same faith and observe the same values? Or will we negotiate ways to preserve and protect differences in faith while seeking to overcome differences that divide and reflect injustice?

What Do Family Values Value?

Religious people differ among themselves on the issue of family values, on theological grounds; they accordingly assume different political positions within and among religious communities.[1] In addition, these differences play themselves out in sometimes sincere, sometimes cynical discourse and action among politicians as makers of public policy who depend on reelection in order to secure their power and influence.

Religious Activism in the Political Arena

With regard to differences among religious people, religious liberals and conservatives alike have acted politically on their religious convictions, including their concerns for the quality of family life, for most of American history. They have focused on abolishing slavery and have reformed working conditions for women and children. They have fought for and against temperance, women's suffrage, gaining and protecting the reproductive rights of women, the teaching of evolution in the public schools, and extending civil rights. They have lobbied both for and against prayer in the public schools. To argue for the separation of religion and politics is to misunderstand the nature of both and indicates a misinterpretation of the separation of religion and state.

One acts politically out of one's deepest convictions, whether these convictions are religious in origin and authority or secular. One may or may not be a fanatic in either case. Furthermore, religious convictions differ drastically even within the same denomination, never mind within the same overarching religious tradition. Thus, today Southern Baptists, Episcopalians, Lutherans, Methodists, Mormons, Presbyterians, and Roman Catholics, among the representatives of other denominations as well, are deeply divided internally over family values within Christendom. Likewise, there is no single monolithic view within Judaism or Islam. Were one to poll Buddhists and Native Americans, one would likely find a diversity of views as well. These differences themselves lead to a healthy check on the establishment of a state religion.

Political activism on religious grounds should not be confused as a violation of the separation of religion and state. On the contrary, religious people, as well as secular people, agitated for the First Amendment guarantee of freedom of religion. As we shall see in the discussion of constitutional rights in chapters 4 and 5, the establishment of a state religion may be one possible consequence of some forms of political activism on behalf of religious convictions. Nevertheless, political activism on the part of religious citizens needs to be critically analyzed, issue by issue, in order to distinguish between the establishment of a state religion and the free exercise of religion, also a constitutional right.

Within the context of religious diversity, the concept *family values* holds different meanings for different religious groups, as well as for secular groups. Many religious conservatives, as well as their religious and secular opponents, identify the concept *family values* with support for prayer in the public schools and control over curricula within the public schools, among other issues presently subject to controversy. These controversies further erupt over the issue of gender and relate directly to the status of women, for example, abortion, control over reproduction, contending theological views of male-female relations within the family, pornography, the legal status of same-sex relations, normative family structure, and pension plans for women who work exclusively in the home.

For other religious people, including conservatives, liberals, and those seeking an alternative to both, the question is not whether to cherish and uphold family life. Rather the question is: How do we best sustain just and decent lives for *all* individual family members, given differences in religious and political creeds, culture, race, ethnicity, class, and sexual preference? People on the different sides of these many issues, who narrowly define religion, often fail to consider the very significant differences among religious people themselves.

Much of what drives contention over family values arises out of legitimate concern for children and from substantive disagreement over cultural norms. Some of this contention also unfortunately represents crass manipulation of these legitimate concerns and fears among voters by politicians seeking to achieve power. Just as we cannot separate religion and politics from one another, so we cannot avoid politicians who co-opt religious concerns for corrupt religious and political ends.

Parents are rightly concerned for the safety, health, education, and well-being of their children. Contention arises over issues of where to draw the line and who should control the family. In contrast to Christians concerned with preserving very specific family patterns out of an exclusive concern for their own children, many Christian activists, regardless of whether they are parents or not, extend this concern to *all* children, as well as to adult family members victimized by domestic abuse. Some Christians focus more exclusively on the present and the near future, whereas others, concerned for the long-range future as well, link violence in the home, violence in the streets, militarism, and systemic violence with environmental abuse. In short, depending on the context, all of these concerns qualify as family values.

Political Exploitation of Family Values

In the midst of this contention politicians from both parties have on occasion addressed parental fears and concerns in less than honorable ways for their own gain. Such political opportunism makes it very difficult to distinguish substantive debate from politicians doing whatever it takes at the moment to get the predominantly white, often socially conservative, middle-class vote. Our leaders often follow momentary trends reflected in interminable poll taking rather than lead the country with a view to the present and future well-being of all its citizenry.

The intertwining of substantive religious and political differences over family values with political exploitation forces a number of questions: How does one distinguish political manipulation from substantive debate? How, for example, are we to read Marilyn Quayle's critique of feminism and her appeal to Murphy Brown to get to know Major Dad during the 1992 Republican convention? Is she sincerely concerned for the well-being of all families, or is she presenting a litmus test of religious and moral respectability, narrowly defined, that a family must pass in order to count as a family in her worldview? Or, for another example, is President Clinton's characteristic oratorical identification of the nation as an all-inclusive family, all members of which stand in covenantal relation to one another, genuinely felt or a rhetorical ploy? And if sincere, what does it mean regarding limits to government intervention, as well as positive programs that relieve the suffering of poor families? In either case, provided one can distinguish between political maneuvering and substantive differences, how can substantive debate take place in spite of political manipulation so that we might negotiate serious resolution to this conflict?

There are no simple answers to the question of how to distinguish political manipulation from substantive debate that reflects real differences in values. Making such a distinction becomes all the more difficult, considering that virtually all of us are subject to mixed and confused motivations not entirely known even to ourselves, a condition understood from a Christian theological perspective as human vulnerability to sin. Nevertheless, in regard to the question of distinguishing between political opportunism and substantive difference, the biblical injunction that "thus you will know them by their fruits" (Matthew 7:20) provides a good starting point. The difference between a Carter administration conference on the family and Pat Robertson's infamous vilification of feminism illustrates this point well.

The 1980 White House Conference on Families, called by then President Jimmy Carter, appears to be one of the first conferences to recognize officially the extent to which family life has dramatically changed in light of the changing role of women in American society. Though women's movement into the public work force was hardly new in this century, the '70s in particular saw what was to be only the beginning of a major surge in the number of women entering the public arena.[2] The Conference committee notes, "American Society is dynamic and constantly changing. The roles and structure of families [and their] individual family members are growing, adapting, and evolving in new and different ways."[3] While not always sanguine about the future for families, the report affirms structural variety for family life and does not blame women as somehow the perpetrators of the destruction of families; on the contrary, it assumes that changing family structure can be beneficial as well as deleterious.

This attitude contrasts dramatically with Pat Robertson's description of feminism as the destroyer of family values during the 1992 Republican convention and later in a fund-raising letter. To be more precise, feminism constitutes "a socialist, anti-family, political movement that encourages women to leave their husbands, kill their children, practice witchcraft, destroy capitalism, and become lesbians."[4] Another evangelical noted in response to Robertson that such talk, while perhaps effective in political fund-raising in certain quarters, "fail[s] to take responsibility for . . . the way that verbal violence and hate talk are precursors to physical violence" (Wallis, 108).

These remarks provide clues useful to making distinctions between political manipulation and substantive debate, namely, the demonization of one's opponents for economic and political gain. Robertson demonizes his perceived opponents by engaging in demagoguery. Moreover, he engages in this kind of polemic because it will result in economic gain and increased political power, thereby benefiting him personally as well as his cause. That Robertson successfully appeals to deep-seated hatreds and fears rather than to reason makes him not the only one responsible for his success, however. Those who hear and are persuaded, as well as those who hear, disagree, but remain silent, become complicit in the damage he elicits. Robertson's speech parallels similar polemic vilifying blacks who strove for civil rights in a previous era, with similar consequences. Just as racist rhetoric further fuels racial hatred that reinforces racial violence, so Robertson's demonization of feminists not only reflects but further elicits misogyny among men and women alike, a misogyny that only further reinforces violence against women. These are hardly the kinds of fruits Christians should seek to cultivate.

Demagoguery for personal gain notwithstanding, substantive debate and dialogue are taking place in a variety of contexts, though not often enough. At stake are not only conflicting views of what *family* and *family values* mean, but also who gets to define the issues themselves. How we sustain, promote, and widen substantive engagement with the issues to include more voices, particularly the voices of the dispossessed, constitutes a difficult and demanding task. Nevertheless, the outcome of the struggle over what counts as family, at any given point in time, determines what family values value. Thus the most crucial question is: Who gets to decide?

Who Gets to Decide?

The issue of who is consulted, represented, and included in the political processes that ultimately determine public policies that shape family life stands at the heart of any substantive debate and dialogue on family values. For substantive debate and dialogue to occur, for serious reform with justice to occur, those who will feel the impact of policy making must have a say in the policy made. Active involvement reflecting multiple perspectives is crucial to genuine democracy, as well as to the lives of those affected by public policy.

Including multiple perspectives has serious theological implications as well. Critical, comparative analysis of two recently published books on politics in the United States from a Christian perspective illustrate this point nicely. Taken together, these books serve as a microcosm of present, ongoing debates. The way each author views the community to which he holds himself accountable provides a window into the very real differences among religious people concerned for the quality of family life in this country.

Though both authors share much in common as evangelical Protestants, they differ drastically on the issue of who gets to decide what counts as family and what or whom family values value. As we shall see, this difference over the power to decide has serious theological and political consequences.

Both *Politically Incorrect*, written by Ralph Reed, and *The Soul of Politics*, written by Jim Wallis, hit the bookstores in 1994. Reed, who holds a doctorate in American history from Emory University, cofounded with Pat Robertson the Christian Coalition, a coalition of conservative religious groups that is predominantly but not exclusively Protestant, that numbers among its supporters Jerry Falwell and James Dobson, along with their respective organizations, all of whom seek political reform commensurate with their interpretation of traditional Christian family values. The Coalition has also sought to align itself politically with morally conservative Roman Catholic and Jewish groups. Rank-and-file members of the Coalition tend to be middle-class Anglo-American Protestants. At this point in history the Coalition has found its political home almost exclusively in the Republican Party, though not without tension and conflict with other Republicans.

By contrast, Wallis, a graduate of Trinity Evangelical Divinity School, founded and heads Sojourners, an activist group that networks with other religious and political activist groups seeking reform in the name of social and environmental justice. As with the Christian Coalition, the quality of family life is a major concern, though this concern shapes the identity of Sojourners in ways that differ distinctively from the Christian Coalition. Sojourners, like the Christian Coalition, is predominantly evangelical Protestant in its membership though, also like the Coalition, it forms alliances across religious traditions. Unlike the Christian Coalition these alliances include Muslim and Native American groups as well as Roman Catholic and Jewish groups. Moreover, rank-and-file members are ethnically, racially, and culturally diverse, as well as more likely to be drawn from low-income and no-income economic classes. At first glance the Democratic Party would appear to be politically and philosophically more amenable to some of the concerns and goals of Sojourners than the Republican Party. The distinctiveness of Sojourners, however, lies in its anti-authoritarian commitment to a decentralization of political and religious decision-making processes, with special priority for including poor people in these processes. This radical decentralizing of power by definition places Sojourners in tension with all establishment politics, particularly the hierarchical party politics characteristic of both major political parties.

Politically Incorrect and *The Soul of Politics*, taken together, are almost as fascinating for their commonalities as for their differences. For example, both books reveal their authors to be extremely bright, articulate, religiously committed white males possessed of extraordinary political savvy and organizational brilliance who launch very clear, persuasive cases for their agendas. As self-identified evangelical Protestants both authors appeal to scripture as authoritative in some fashion, though not necessarily to be taken literally or to be taken as infallible. Evangelical Protestantism informs their respective positions in a variety of other ways as well. Both authors sound a prophetic alarm: economic, political, and social structures have deteriorated to such an extent, as characterized by violence, political and moral bankruptcy, cultural degeneration, and personal irresponsibility, that the country faces imminent self-destruction.

Neither the traditional political parties nor politics as we presently know them in any form can resolve this crisis. Both Reed and Wallis invite the reader to consider a third alternative to traditional political liberalism and traditional political conservatism. In characteristically evangelical fashion both Reed and Wallis call for an experience of transformation that is at once personal and communal, as well as spiritual and political. Both authors argue that such transformation is necessary to end ongoing disaster and to restore the country to wholeness. Both authors further place their hopes in grassroots movements as the arena for communal or social transformation; they stress that grassroots movements, working across both political parties rather than forming a third political party, have already begun to effect needed social change.

In short, both books are pragmatically oriented manifestos, argued on theological grounds, that call for political activism, based on religious conviction. Both Reed and Wallis represent movements rooted in an American history of socioreligious reform. Wallis's *The Soul of Politics* is reminiscent of Walter Rauschenbusch's *A Theology for the Social Gospel* (1907).[5] Reed explicitly positions the Christian Coalition as a direct descendant of the Social Gospel movement (1870–1918), though his claim is not to my mind persuasive (151, 264). In regard to both books an attentive reader senses an urgency that both authors' willingness to be self-critical as well as critical of culture bespeaks their deeply held convictions.

Two Different Views of Democracy

Against this backdrop of commonality the differences are astonishing. They are numerous as well. One difference is particularly relevant to a discussion of what counts as family, what family values value, and who gets to decide. This difference lies in the communities that most concern Reed and Wallis, with special reference to what afflicts them.

The full title of Reed's book carries within the thesis he seeks to argue, namely, *Mainstream Values Are No Longer Politically Incorrect: The Emerging Faith Factor in American Politics*. Reed claims that fundamentalists and evangelicals, taken together as religious conservatives, have suffered discrimination and religious prejudice on a par with the discrimination and bigotry experienced in this country by African Americans. Rejecting categories like the "religious right," he refers to the religious conservatives he represents as a "pro-family movement" and the "people of faith." He simultaneously claims that in spite of the status of his constituency as outsiders because of their religious convictions, the values of the people of faith nevertheless are now and always have been mainstream American values, namely, family values, biblically grounded.

Reed acknowledges that the movement he represents is populated predominantly, almost exclusively, by whites and is strongly critical of the history of racism that characterizes white fundamentalist and evangelical communities, institutions, and social movements, particularly in the South. He moreover makes a concerted effort to rectify this past by appealing directly to racial and ethnic minorities, which he describes as uniformly conservative, to make common cause with him by joining the movement. In addition to seeking more racial and ethnic diversity, he considers the movement to be religiously ecumenical, though he consistently attacks New Age spiritualism and refers to Islam only with respect to terrorism. He further makes direct appeal to a potential working-class constituency as well. In respect to all racial, religious, and class diversity, Reed's aim is to include previously excluded groups, based on commonly held values that Reed claims to be mainstream. By *mainstream* he means predominantly, though not exclusively, values that exemplify the familial and social arrangements and the aspirations of upwardly mobile working-class and middle-class white consumers.

While self-references like *pro-family movement* are troubling enough in their implication that anyone not part of the movement is anti-family, his self-definition as *people of faith* is even more disturbing for its theological implications. Reed speaks as if he were speaking for all people who by God's grace seek to place their trust in God and seek to be loyal to God. Wallis's book serves as ample evidence that Reed assuredly does not speak for all people of faith. Because Reed connects *people of faith* directly with conservative religion (predominantly conservative Christianity), he furthermore implies that if one is not conservative, one is not a person of faith. This is simply not true; many religious conservatives do not agree with him.

Reed is no doubt sincere in his intentions to represent certain forms of monotheistic faith, and he speaks clearly, if not always persuasively, on behalf of the concerns of their adherents. There are, however, many forms of monotheistic faith, as well as many faiths, secular as well as religious, for which he does not speak. His reference to *people of faith* as if it were comprehensive in scope is thus misleading.

Theological problems exist as well. Institutional affiliation alone does not make one a person of faith. The concept of *People of faith* as Reed portrays it carries a theological presumptuousness that includes, among other things, lack of sufficient awareness of the vulnerability of the faithful to sin, particularly the sinfulness of knowing precisely who are and who are not people of faith. As a Christian who struggles daily with a vulnerability to faithlessness and as a theologian for whom such issues are more than simply personal, I find this lack of awareness troubling in its oversimplification of faith and of people. A human presumption to know who is and who is not a person of faith leads easily to idolatry, for it assumes a position that only God can assume. This tendency to oversimplify further permeates Reed's critique of culture and his vision for America, even as it characterizes much of the political and theological thought of the Christian Coalition and the pro-family movement as a whole.

In striking contrast to Reed's allegedly mainstream people of faith, Wallis's movement places the struggles of the poverty-stricken and the outcast at the center of his concern, though Wallis connects their victimization and suffering to a variety of forms of violence, extending throughout the public arena and including environmental destruction. While clearly granting the needs of the poor priority, Wallis celebrates a broad range of differences, in contrast to Reed, who seeks to assimilate differences into a preexisting mainstream culture. Wallis cultivates diversity from the streets of urban ghettos to the rural backwaters of third world countries through a highly participatory democracy characteristic of gang summits and base communities.

Wallis approaches community by establishing multicultural coalitions among self-structured and self-directed groups, who resolve disagreement within and among the groups through intense, sustained, nonviolent negotiation among all parties involved. What theologically unites these highly fluid, pluralistic networks and prevents them from dissolving into moral relativism for Wallis is the *imago Dei* (image of God), borne by all humans. He further connects the image of God to the biblical hope for redemption—a redemption of the earth and all its kind, as well as the redemption of humans—and justice, especially for the dispossessed. In contrast to *people of faith*, Wallis speaks of the *people of God*, by which he means everybody past, present, and future, bound by their having been created from the earth to other creatures and to the earth, as well as to God. The intense diversity he cultivates within the movement itself, in other words, his practice of participatory democracy, prevents this cosmic vision from degenerating into vague abstraction.

People who do not share Wallis's conviction that humans are created in the image of God, either because they are not religious or because their religion does not depend on the existence of a god, may find his theology dissatisfying, discomfiting, or distasteful. Nevertheless, Wallis's view of political activism, in contrast to Reed's, does not require agreement on matters of religious faith; rather it requires working in partnership with poor people for social transformation that does justice for all. Though Wallis calls for a spiritual renewal, he does not define participation in terms of adherence to particular kinds of religious faith.

Wallis's point is to disrupt dichotomies like "mainstream" as opposed to "margin," and "affluent" as opposed to "poor," in favor of a radically participatory, highly decentralized democracy that is always in the process of defining itself. Thus, in contrast to Reed, Wallis does not seek to integrate racially marginalized people into a mainstream. From Wallis's perspective, this kind of racial integration is just another word for assimilation to white upper- and upper-middle-class values in support of preserving their political and cultural dominance. The personal cost is a loss of the distinctiveness of one's cultural identity and values. The social cost is that oppressive systems of power remain in place. Wallis seeks instead a complete restructuring of human social and spiritual life, a restructuring, the results of which cannot by definition be foreseen in advance, since everyone has a say in remaking the power structure as we go. *People of God*, as employed by Wallis, in contrast to the more divisive *people of faith*, as employed by Reed, sustains diversity within communities, as well as across them.

The People of Faith and the People of God

Christian traditions carry within them a potential tension between what is distinctive to Christian identity, namely, faith in God through Jesus Christ—a faith not all people share—and the injunctions to love other human beings regardless of whether they are neighbors, strangers, or enemies and, therefore, regardless of whether they share the same faith or even any particularly religious faith. Out of this tension the temptation arises to assert the priority of Christian doctrine and group membership over Christian practice. The difference between *people of faith* and *people of God* demonstrates this tension well. Were the people of faith to accomplish everything on their political agenda, whole groups of people would be excluded from the political decision-making processes characteristic of genuine democracy, a goal we have yet to attain. By contrast, a radical comprehension of what it means to be created in the image of God makes excluding disagreeable neighbors, strangers, and enemies from the decision-making processes that influence their lives a dishonoring of God.

As Christians, then, we need to ask ourselves which view of community is more commensurate with Christian faith and practice. In addition, as citizens of the United States we also need to ask which community stands more in accord with a genuine democracy.

The people of God are God's people irrespective of their faith or lack of it, and the image of God they bear requires honor regardless of their views, including the view that there is no God. The people of faith, as Reed represents them, comprise a much narrower community, formed along more doctrinal lines. The people of God stand in relation to one another as full partners, irrespective of their differences, even when these differences include serious substantive conflict with one another. The people of faith as portrayed by Reed have a blueprint they seek to enact, that if enacted, restricts the rights of those with whom the people of faith disagree in ways that do not allow for dissent, negotiation, or equal partnership.

The people of God include the pro-family movement as partners in the processes of resolving dispute over differences in family values. However, I do not see the people of faith welcoming poverty-stricken children, gays and lesbians, or pro-choice women to enter into dialogue with them. The authoritarian, antihomosexual, and antiabortion values the people of faith espouse preclude negotiation. In all fairness, it is likewise not at all clear that everyone else included in the people of God would necessarily be as willing to sit down with one another or with the Christian Coalition to work through the problems we confront, as Wallis is willing to invite them to do. Nevertheless, honoring the image of God in each and every human provides an excellent starting place for setting up negotiations.

Conclusion

What do family values value? Who gets to decide? The image of God establishes God at the center of a kinship shared among all human beings. Thus, humankind as the people of God, past, present, and future, counts as family. This kinship establishes a human responsibility to value all particular families within the human family, irrespective of the structure, values, or circumstances of any given family. To value families other than one's own further requires the input and empowerment of those most affected by any given decision-making process. To value one's own particular family means honoring the image of God each family member bears. In short, the image of God requires of Christians that we seek the good of each and every member of the human family for the future as well as the present.

God stands at the center of this kinship. As a primary condition for human existence as human, the image of God makes human relationship with God the central relationship overriding all others, including particular family relations. The centrality of this relationship denies us the elevation of our finite values, including family values, to the status of moral absolutes, and reminds us that even the good we seek is limited by our own finitude. This limitation only further reinforces the need for the full participation of everyone affected in the decision-making processes that govern family life.

What do family values value? Whatever codes we seek to formulate must be provisional and in direct response to the changing material conditions families confront, with special attention to the impact of domestic violence, gender, racial, and ethnic bias, and prejudice against the poor. So, for example, in the case of prejudice against the poor, the traditional nuclear family headed by a single breadwinner is for the most part restricted to predominantly white, upper and upper-middle classes because of the level of affluence required to sustain this arrangement. This affluence depends in turn partly on underpaid and sometimes illegal labor of housekeepers, nannies, and yard workers that may be destructive to the stability of the laborers' families. In light of this practice, we become hypocrites when we support tough laws that withhold health care, welfare, and public education from the children of illegal immigrants.

Who gets to decide? Most important, in a genuine democracy the "we" who are doing all this negotiating and debating needs to include at some level everybody involved in and affected by the negotiations. Radical, participatory democracy requires the kind of grassroots organization and energy reflected by Sojourners. In other words, answering the question of what counts as family by affirming multiple family patterns carries with it the responsibility to involve people from every possible family configuration in the public processes that determine the policies that shape their lives. Among the people of God, those who are at greatest risk have the highest priority for consideration in regard to making social policy. The issue thus becomes how to organize.

The Genesis account of creation in the image of God serves as only the beginning of Christian teaching on what it means to be human in relation to God, to one another, and to the earth, however. What does the image of God have to do with cherishing our differences and forming the kinds of particular relations within our common humanity that foster justice? According to the Genesis accounts, God created humans as different from one another. How Christians interpret the element of difference in the creation narratives also plays a major role in what family means, where freedom lies, and who gets to decide.

3

Thinking Difference
Differently

If what God did during the first seven days of creation establishes the connections among all creatures and between the human family and God (Genesis 1:1–2:4), the story of Adam and Eve connects the human family directly to the earth and to one another (Genesis 2:4–3:24). After all, God creates Adam from the earth and the Hebrew word *'ādām* itself is a play on words meaning both "human," without reference to gender, and "dirt creature." Most important, the story focuses on the significance of difference itself: the difference between the human creature Adam and the other creatures, the difference between Adam and God, and differences among human beings. While without difference there would assuredly be no conflict, without it there would be no possibility for relationship either. Without it there could be no possibility for covenant.[1]

Genesis 2:4–3:24 and Difference

The first difference the human creature confronts is the difference between human beings and other kinds of creatures. Their common status as creatures notwithstanding, the human lacks enough commonality with the other creatures to find the kind of intimacy and partnership that the human creature seeks. This difference forces the human to appeal to God for a more fitting companion.

The difference between God and Adam constitutes a second, more subtle difference. Clearly Adam not only finds the other creatures inadequate companions, but God likewise cannot or does not sufficiently

perform this role either. After all, if relationship with God fulfilled everything the human creature needed and desired, why would God make another, different, human companion? Nowhere in the text does the narrator make explicit specifically what is missing either in the relationship
between the dirt creature and the other creatures or in the relationship
with God; rather, what is missing is implied. God makes another creature,
for it is not good for the first one to be alone. God makes the second creature from the first so that the first can recognize it as "bone of my bones
and flesh of my flesh" (Genesis 2:23), in other words, they are alike. Nevertheless, they are sufficiently different such that hereinafter future generations will leave their homes of origin to form new unions. Thus God
initially intended the dirt creature, the first human, to form equal partnership with someone both sufficiently like the dirt creature to be equal
and sufficiently different for them to be in relationship as partners.

Equality and partnership bring us to the third difference. When God
creates Eve from Adam's rib, God creates a different human being. The
second human being differs not only in gender, an issue that I shall
shortly pursue at length, but also in other ways—how God creates her,
how she responds to moral dilemmas, and how she is connected to future
human life. God creates her from the heretofore undifferentiated human
dirt creature, rather than as an altogether different kind of creature. This
at once binds the two subsequent creatures to each other even as it distinguishes them from each other. Furthermore, the undifferentiated dirt
creature, Adam, plays at best a passive role in the process; her creation is
all God's doing.

Adam's initial passivity has implications for the future; later in the
garden, when Eve encounters the serpent who persuades her to take the
fruit and eat it, the encounter serves as a contrast with her subsequent
proffering of the fruit to Adam. Just as Adam the human is passive in the
creation of Eve, likewise Adam, the man, is passive in acquiring the
knowledge of good and evil that introduces sin and death into human life.
The text indicates that in contrast to Eve, Adam offers no resistance, requires no persuasion; succumbs to no seduction. He simply takes the offered fruit and eats. Thus Eve differs from Adam in her willingness to engage in moral reasoning, for better or for worse. Last but not least, the
woman differs from the man in regard to the future. Upon recognizing
her as related to him, Adam calls out to her as Eve, which translates as the
bearer or mother of life. Her appearance on the scene marks the first
glimmer of the possibility in Adam's mind of a human future, based on
human interaction—one that will require for future generations leaving
one's father and mother and cleaving to new partners (Genesis 2:24). In

one symbolic event human commonality and difference, joyously oriented toward an unknown future, are born.

In Genesis 2—3, Adam the dirt creature, dirt being a connection to the earth all humans share, becomes two different but related creatures, man and woman, and the woman becomes Eve, the bearer of life. Placed in the context of Genesis 1:26–28 (the first reference to God's creation of humankind), the story of Adam and Eve casts a richer light on more precisely how humans are created in the image of God. From a Trinitarian perspective, the story of Adam and Eve, understood more abstractly as the story of the creation of difference in relationship, tells us that God requires differentiation and relation as well, not only within God's own internal life and creativity, but externally as a fundamental characteristic of God's creating and redeeming activity in the world. Because the divine life requires differentiation within relationship, to be created in the image of God means that God intends humans for relation with God, with other humans, and with the rest of God's creation.

In other words, the story of Adam and Eve is about more than the creation of gender difference. As the story of the first human family, it narrates human differentiation within relationship in terms of faithfulness and ultimately betrayal, in terms of both responsibility and freedom. The story of the creation and fall of Adam and Eve focuses on faithfulness to and betrayal of other creatures and God, as well as human faithfulness to and betrayal of one another. It sets up early on an enduring tension between obligations to others and individual freedom. It clarifies theologically that the image of God borne by all humans is borne, as in the case of God, in relationship with others rather than in isolation from them.

What I have offered here is only one possible interpretation of Genesis 2—3. Dependent on a number of other interpretations, my interpretation remains relatively abstract in regard to details, and at points it obviously contradicts more conventional interpretations.[2] Until now I have for the most part avoided the issue of gender difference. My point is that while this story is very obviously about gender, one can also read the narrative as a story about the nature and significance of difference itself, for which gender difference is a case study, so to speak. In this chapter I plan to explore the issue of gender difference at some length, though not only in its own right, but also in relation to other issues. Gender difference, how it emerges, and how it manifests itself in family life involves making certain fundamental distinctions and acknowledging certain tensions important to understanding how other differences arise in a wider society or culture as well as within the family. In other words, gender difference provides only one case study of the dynamics of difference. Without reference to all significant differences that characterize the uniqueness of every human identity, any discussion of how to sustain a radical, pluralistic democracy that can negotiate internal conflict on family issues is severely limited.

Genesis and Gender

From biblical times to the present, Christian theologians and ministers have conventionally interpreted the story of the creation of Adam and Eve as divine authorization for the subordination of women to men. After all Eve is created second; her existence is derived from Adam's by virtue of having been created from him rather than separately from the dirt as he was. She is created at his request for the purpose of helping him in his projects, named by him like the other creatures, and cursed by God to be ruled by him.[3] This kind of interpretation fails to take into account the self-interest and propensity to sexism of some male interpreters.

In contrast to this view, there is a long-standing historical tradition of interpretation, also male, influenced by Plato's creation story in the *Timaeus,* that sees Adam, prior to the creation of Eve, as human in a generic sense, not sexed because human sexuality cannot occur until there is more than one human. For theologians representing this tradition of interpretation, the creation of Eve is the creation of sexual differentiation and, thereby, the creation of the possibility for both human relationship and human procreation. Furthermore, the creation of Eve from Adam's rib or side signifies for this tradition that the two are equal partners, who as sexual beings are created simultaneously.[4] While this interpretation can be used as a way of privileging heterosexuality, a point to which I shall return, my point here is that within the history of biblical interpretation, dominated as it has been by male interpreters, there is disagreement among men over the meaning of the text.

More recently women biblical scholars and theologians have focused on this narrative, and they too differ with one another on whether to interpret it as a story justifying inequality or equality. For many women, the narrative, interpreted as a story of inequality, serves as grounds for leaving the church. Others, who interpret the same account as one of equality, call the church to repent its sexism. The interpretations I find most persuasive and fascinating are the ones that stress sexual equality as God's intention, an equality derailed by sin. From this perspective, God's pronouncement that Eve would be ruled by Adam was a foreshadowing that sexism itself is sinful, rather than a divine validation of male dominance (Trible, 80–81).

All this disagreement over meaning exemplifies the extent to which scripture can be interpreted in multiple ways by readers who bring values, assumptions, and interests to these texts, such that they render a neutral reading impossible. Furthermore, the interpretations themselves have enormous consequences both in determining human actions and in justifying them after the fact. The idea that sacred text is subject to multiple, sometimes conflicting interpretation is hardly new to theologians, biblical scholars, clergy, and many Christian laypeople. John Calvin himself understood that apprehending a text as divine revelation required the Holy Spirit operating not only within the text, but also within the reader. Without the operation of the Spirit within the person and the text, the text itself was dead.[5] In more modern terms conflict over meaning suggests that we test our interpretations out publicly, together in prayerful dialogue, in accordance with what we understand to be overarching convictions of our faith. So, for example, we would interpret scripture in light of the conviction that all humans are created in the image of God, as manifested in the commandments to love God and neighbor.[6] Thus, biblical interpretation can itself be an exercise in participatory democracy, provided everyone concerned gets to be involved and the right to dissent is protected.

The Fatherhood of Men and the Motherhood of Everybody

Chapter 2 analyzed how Christians select and interpret biblical narrative according to different theological traditions. Conflict emerging out of these differing traditions becomes especially acute when it comes to trying to understand the theological implications of what it means to be parents. Not only do Christians contend over the meaning of the creation of Adam and Eve, but they turn to other biblical resources for understanding what it means to be mothers and fathers as well. Theologians from across the spectrum come to contrary and conflicting conclusions as a result. A comparison of the positions of religious conservative Stu Weber and religious progressive Bonnie Miller-McLemore indicates dramatically the difference one's theology makes when Christians seek to understand what it means to be parents.

Conventional interpretation of the creation of Adam and Eve has played a central role in the theology shaping and justifying the conceptions of family that characterize Christians active in the pro-family movement. The theology of Stu Weber serves as a case in point. A former Green Beret and Vietnam veteran, Weber, along with his wife, Linda, cofounded the Good Shepherd Community Church in Oregon. Together they travel throughout the countryside speaking at FamilyLife marriage and parenting conferences. Weber formulates his theological position in *Tender Warrior: God's Intention for a Man*, further subtitled as *Every Man's Purpose, Every Woman's Dream, Every Child's Hope.* On the jacket cover Dr. Robert Lewis, pastor of the Fellowship Bible Church in Little Rock, Arkansas, describes *Tender Warrior* as a "soul-stirring masculine manifesto."

As a masculine manifesto it calls Christian men to their duties and responsibilities to their families. Weber acknowledges the validity of what he understands to be feminist critique of male failure to live up to the responsibilities of fatherhood, as well as the validity of the men's movement in its search for better forms of masculinity and better relations among men, as characterized by Robert Bly's *Iron John*.[7] From Weber's perspective, however, what lies at the heart of cultural and social crisis is the failure of men to assume their God-ordained role as providers and heads of the household. Instead men have abandoned, abused, misunderstood, or neglected their wives and children. Weber argues alternatively for a specifically Christian masculinity. He appeals to the story of Adam and Eve, the story of David and Jonathan, the New Testament passages enjoining wives to submit to their husbands, and the masculinity of Christ as authoritative for his position.

The chief characteristics of Christian masculinity, as implied in the title, are toughness and tenderness necessary to lead effectively a two-parent, nuclear family. Christian men are tender warriors who lead not because they are superior to women in value. Rather, from Weber's perspective, God proclaims throughout scripture, from the Genesis account to the New Testament, leadership both in the home and in the public arena to be men's job. Indeed this job defines them as men. This leadership not only entails providing for the family and assuming final responsibility for all family decisions it also includes involvement with child rearing insofar as possible, given public commitments. It further requires practiced sensitivity to gender difference, which Weber understands to be grounded in nature, as well as ordained by God. Sensitivity to gender difference according to Weber involves learning to speak "woman." Learning to speak "woman" entails making women feel special, cutting them slack when they are at the mercy of their hormones, acknowledging their special gifts as the ones who are oriented toward relationship rather than toward accomplishing goals, and under no circumstances responding to them abusively. In respect to the children it involves bringing them up according to their gender as God the father brought up his child with a love that is willing to sacrifice everything including one's own child if duty requires it. For Weber this personally meant having to suspend his immediate child-rearing responsibilities when called to serve in Vietnam.

nily forms the base of a pyramid that represents a
tical and social hierarchy. Real men not only play
families as heads of the household, they are also
edient citizens who patriotically serve their coun-
their congregations. All these activities exemplify
ce to God. This strong commitment to the public
omestic one requires cultivating a deep loyalty to
r spends considerable time addressing male friend-
biblical story of David and Jonathan, though there
ling friendship between males and females. Weber
alty is highly personal as well as principled and is
s abroad as well as confronting problems at home.
entification of human fatherhood with the father-
in loyalty to Christ as the truest most complete im-
athentic masculinity. In other words, the significant
nd through God Christ, is masculinity. For Weber
fathers or not, are identified through their divinely
ith divine masculinity itself. Their role is to serve as
fathers in public life, if not always domestic life.

The strength of Weber's position lies in his focus on one of the major problems families confront, namely, neglect and abandonment by fathers and husbands. This focus manifests itself in the sincerity of his concern for the well-being of families, the energy he puts into reeducating
men to be more responsible in all facets of their existence, and his
adamant rejection of violence in the home in any form. Nevertheless, his
position suffers serious problems—as much from what he does not take
into consideration as from what he does consider.

In terms of what Weber does consider, his theology is first and foremost a monument to idolatry. The status he grants masculinity, although
his view of it is hardly stereotypically macho, places it at the definitive
center of who God is. In other words, Weber legitimates male leadership
and the subordination of women to that leadership, both inside and outside the home, by identifying men with his own take on the masculinity
exemplified in the maleness of Christ and the fatherhood of God. In addition, by identifying leadership both in the home and in the public arena
so definitively and exclusively with masculinity, he idolizes the male-
headed nuclear family and loyalty to country as well.

Idolizing maleness as constitutive of the divine flies in the face of the
prohibition against making graven images "in the form of any figure—
the likeness of male or female" (Deuteronomy 4:16), not to mention

Jesus' injunction to call no man father (Matthew 23:9). Idolizing patriotism and the family follows in the same vein. Both his view of patriotism
and his conception of the family disregard the ambiguity of the status of
both civil and family connections found throughout the New Testament.
For example, the earliest followers of Jesus refused to serve in the Roman
military, one of the reasons for which they were persecuted. Furthermore, for some of the earliest followers, notably the disciples, following
Jesus meant giving up any primacy of family ties. These various forms of
idolatry that permeate Weber's position exemplify a self-serving use of
scripture, however unintended, to justify power arrangements from
which he as male directly benefits.

Weber's goal of converting men to taking responsibility for their involvement in reproductive life as well as productive life is laudable. He
unfortunately seeks to achieve this goal on grounds that are not only theologically dubious, but socially detrimental to women as family members,
as workers, as political leaders, and as active participants and leaders in
their congregations and denominations. No doubt a number of women
find Weber's view of domestic and public life satisfactory. Certainly the
position he takes encourages men to assume more responsibility for economic provision for the family and encourages a relative respect for, sensitivity to, and appreciation of women as feminine beings.

If women wish to enter into such arrangements, they should be free
to do so. Women should be cognizant of the risks involved, however. For
example, what happens when a husband is unable for reasons beyond his
control to make economic provision? Suppose he gets laid off by his place
of employment, or is injured and has little or no disability compensation?
In addition, the respect, sensitivity, and appreciation toward women that
Weber espouses depends heavily on relegating them as feminine beings
to the realm of caretaker without consideration for other kinds of traits
and aspirations according to which women might wish to define themselves.

In regard to those women who reject the role Weber espouses for
them, neither they nor Weber live solely in their own families or in closed
religious communities. Weber's view of male domination in the public
arena affects this arena, including the women active within it, as well as
those who seek to enter it. That masculinity for Weber includes no reference to friendships between men and women implies that women are
not only excluded from public leadership, but also primarily valued
largely if not exclusively for their sexuality and potential reproductive ca-
pacities. Men who hold such views create yet one more handicap for the
women who have to work with them in the public arena.

Similar criticisms can be made on behalf of homosexual men and women, extended families, single-parent families, divorced and remarried families, and single people, regardless of their sexual preference, who have never married. Nowhere in *Tender Warrior* does Weber address any of these issues beyond how to re-create the nuclear family. Heterosexuality resulting in marriage and preferably children, in the form of a nuclear family, is simply assumed to be the divinely ordained norm for human existence. There are other problems as well—among them Weber's naiveté regarding domestic abuse (essentially, "just say no") and his inattention to what it means when both parents in a nuclear family work outside the home while rearing their children.

Weber and those who share his views have constitutional rights to hold such views; they likewise have the right to seek to persuade others to join their cause. They have no right, however, to impose legislation that impinges on the freedom directly or indirectly of those who disagree. So, for example, seeking to dismantle the Legal Services Corporation because it assists poverty-stricken women who seek divorce or proposing to require by law the notification of the father of a fetus prior to an abortion goes beyond persuasion to an infringement of the rights of others (Reed, 99–100, 228). Insofar as this kind of legislation reflects specific religious convictions regarding divorce and abortion, it privileges one form of religious conviction and practice over other conflicting religious and secular convictions and practices. This privileging not only violates the free exercise of those whose convictions and practices differ, it has the effect, if not the intention, of establishing a state religion.

Most families in this country nevertheless remain two-parent families though in many cases the two parents have been married previously as well. More often than not, both parents work outside the home, by economic necessity, by choice, or by a combination of both. These families face enormous difficulty as parents seek to juggle work outside the home with child-rearing and household responsibilities, civic responsibility, and faithfulness within their religious communities. This juggling is especially complicated by how culture, including Christian traditions, defines gender difference. In the past women in the middle and working classes have had primary responsibility for the care of their children and the home. Entering the public arena for these women means finding decent day care. Unless women hold jobs that support an upper-middle-class lifestyle that includes hiring outside help (an exception, rather than a rule), entering the work force often means holding down two full-time jobs or, where domestic work is shared with the husband, still assuming disproportionate domestic responsibility. Working one-and-one-half to two full-time jobs arises due to a number of reasons. These reasons range from guilt on the part of many mothers for what they perceive to be neglecting their traditional duties, to a sense of obligation because women are often paid less than men and therefore contribute less to overall household expenses, to the refusal of male spouses to share in what is traditionally viewed as women's work.

In her book, *Also a Mother: Work and Family as Theological Dilemma*, Bonnie Miller-McLemore places these difficulties faced by working parents, especially mothers, squarely in a theological context directly relevant to family values. She does not address at length the Genesis account of Adam and Eve. Instead, she locates herself theologically in relation to the story of Orpah, Naomi's other daughter-in-law, the one who in contrast to Ruth returns to the house of her own mother (Ruth 1:14–15). Miller-McLemore asks, as a feminist Christian, what it means today to choose to be a mother and, as a mother, to return to the family and home after working outside it each day. Miller-McLemore focuses at length on mothering from the perspective of actual mothers, as well as from concern with the needs of children.[8] Her book therefore merits extensive attention.

In *Also a Mother: Work and Family as Theological Dilemma*, Miller-McLemore redefines the concept *generativity* from a feminist perspective as a theological as well as developmental category that integrates nurture within the family with productivity in the workplace for both women and men (41–83). *Generativity* refers to nurture, usually in the context of reproduction. Psychoanalyst Erik Erikson adopted the term to refer more specifically to a stage in the later life of an adult when he becomes less concerned with work in the public arena and more concerned with nurturing activities, most often in response to his grandchildren. Erikson assumed that he was speaking of both men and women when he developed the concept.[9]

Miller-McLemore points out that culture historically defines women specifically in terms of generativity throughout their lives, just as it defines men in terms of their productivity in the workplace. To be generative, as she redefines the concept, is to integrate productive labor in the public workplace with reproduction and nurture in the home for both men and women. She accomplishes this task with special attention to meeting the needs of both women who rear children and the children whom they rear. Severely critical of self-sacrificing love as the paradigm for mothering, she redefines "mother" as "the adult who cares" (Miller-McLemore, 172). Mothering, "a caring labor" (174), thus becomes a responsibility to the future to be shared by all adult members of a community (167–72). She is likewise critical of models for work grounded in consumption-oriented definitions of success and based on a family within which fathers have little or no opportunity, encouragement, or responsibility for the nurture of children.

Accordingly, typical contemporary family arrangements still depend too heavily on allocating primary responsibility for nurture to women and primary passion for work in the public arena to men. As she points out, this arrangement not only perpetuates injustice toward women, it destroys or delays until late adulthood, usually when the first grandchild is born at or near retirement, men's development of their own generativity as an exercise of nurture. As a result, both the family and the workplace suffer unnecessary impoverishment, though women in particular suffer the most as unpaid, underdeveloped, overly responsible laborers in both the public and the domestic arenas.

Several factors make this situation of injustice a specifically theological issue for Miller-McLemore: the neglect of the significance of Orpah's return to her own family; the sexism of scripture and of biblical interpretation; the negative role of the church as center for idolizing the family; the positive potential within the church as community where all congregants take on the project of generativity at all stages of life in a variety of different ways; the theological and moral implications of lactation; and the timely interaction of self-sacrifice and self-love necessary to child rearing.

Miller-McLemore skillfully weaves psychological theory and theology together with her own experience of mothering in conscious awareness of the limitations of her location in culture. She is a white, middle-class, professional woman with a keen appreciation for the significance of racial, generational, and to a lesser degree, class and ethnic differences. Her critiques of theory, theology, the church, and feminism are themselves extraordinarily constructive, reflecting her awareness of the ambiguity of her own identity as a Christian feminist practical theologian. The concept of the nurturing self that emerges from her text is not surprisingly a self available both to men and to women. This self is fluid, culturally variable, interdependent with other selves, related to others because it is supremely related to God. This self needs to give and to receive nurture throughout life and to experience the tangible and intangible joys and rewards of productive and, for some women—not all—reproductive labor. She entirely resists any temptation to sever a connection between work outside the home and child rearing, between productive and reproductive labor for both men and women. Moreover, she successfully resists any urge to romanticize or to mystify mothers, children, and work in the public arena.

Miller-McLemore acknowledges the frustrations of child rearing along with concerns to meet the needs of children and concerns to extend a capacity for nurture to men and women irrespective of whether they rear children. She insists on the importance, indeed primacy, of telling and retelling the untold stories of women, in Miller-McLemore's case, the telling of Orpah's story. Most important, she proposes a constructive view of Christian identity as located in generativity, redefined to unite nurture with labor in a context that is at once attuned to the significance of gender difference, while committed to gender equality.

Nevertheless, her treatment of mothering in the context of work does not directly address the situation of families, particularly mothers, plagued by poverty, violence, neglect, or abandonment by other family members, religious communities, and secular institutions. She, like Weber, does not address families other than nuclear families.

This does not diminish the extraordinary contribution she makes in advancing an understanding of the difficulties faced by two-parent families. On the contrary, how to be better parents in any circumstances is a serious issue. Nevertheless, much of the discussion concerning family values focuses too exclusively on issues of gender, as if the most pressing issues families face had to do with how to be better women and men in distinction from one another, rather than with parenthood. Weber's book is typical in this respect.

My own experience as a parent teaches me that parents are made rather than born and that we as a society do a poor job of preparing and supporting adults as parents. It is difficult under the best of circumstances to know how to find that balance that both fosters a child's creativity and sets needed limits commensurate with the child's own temperament and development. It is likewise difficult to find that balance between mother-child relations that validates what are the sometimes conflicting needs of both. This is especially difficult for parents in response to a first child or an only child. As a working mother who shared child-rearing responsibilities with the father of our child insofar as a male-dominated culture of work would permit, I found my own experience greatly confirmed by Miller-McLemore's analysis and undermined by Weber's. Even under optimal circumstances child rearing and working outside the home are extremely difficult.

All the same, Miller-McLemore's representation of family life does not address the full magnitude of the tragedy of what it means to be human, male or female. What does it mean when there is no community, when institutions and interpersonal relationships fail, when work is either not there or not rewarding, when the body breaks down, when the psyche is wounded far beyond simple mending, when one has lost control over one's own agency and yet is somehow responsible? In short, What does it mean when an adult in charge of a family is both severely damaged and damaging? Rearing children by oneself, assuming primary responsibility for elderly family members, having to teach children how to respond to racial and ethnic slurs or humiliation based on gender, parenting in poverty, fleeing for one's safety or the safety of one's children, and being responsible for a family while homeless set the agenda for many parents in this country. For these people the problems Miller-McLemore confronts and the struggle against prevailing norms that she and her family undertake, and others like her including myself, should not be trivialized in any respect; however, they are, after all is said and done, the problems and struggles of one who has a full-time partner who shares her values, one who has productive labor in the public world, one who has chosen to bear and rear children, one who, though she has consciously chosen work in a service profession over the fast track to material success, can be considered by most standards to be materially affluent—a situation Miller-McLemore acknowledges throughout the book.

Both Miller-McLemore and Weber are Christian clergy who seek to extend nurture as a moral virtue to be cultivated and exercised by people who do not necessarily reproduce. Weber seeks to persuade men that fatherhood is at the heart of masculinity, to be exhibited by men in all areas of their lives, whether they themselves are biological fathers or not. Miller-McLemore seeks to persuade everyone that generativity, often restricted to motherhood or accessible to men only in their later lives, is a trait not only available to all adult persons, but also morally required of them as members of a wider community. These claims are particularly crucial to how Christians think about what it means to claim that the church is family, as well as critical to how all citizens of the United States think about what it means to claim that the nation is family. I shall consider each of these claims separately in due course. Note, however, that Weber restricts the exercise of fatherly nurture to men, whereas Miller-McLemore extends motherly nurture to all adults regardless of gender. What does this difference have to say about how we think gender difference itself?

Difference versus Division

In Genesis there is very little content attached to the differences between Adam and Eve in regard to gender. Only when the couple recognizes their nakedness, after they have eaten the fruit, do differences specifically associated with gender appear, and this new awareness reflects sinfulness rather than what God initially intended for humanity. Recognition of their nakedness brings with it shame, the covering of their bodies, and their hiding from God in fear. The text contains no explanation for how nakedness connects to a knowledge of good and evil. Furthermore, the text remains silent as to why shame is a response to nakedness or why nakedness and shame lead to covering the body and hiding from God in fear.

Theologians, preachers, and other biblical interpreters have speculated in a variety of ways. John Calvin, for example, in his commentary on Genesis labors at length over this part of the Genesis account, dismissing any identification of embodiment and sexuality with sin and arguing instead that the covered genitals symbolize an attempt to cover a now corrupted human will.[10] However one construes the connections of a knowledge of good and evil with nakedness, or the progression from nakedness to shame and fear, the progression of events and feelings occurs only after both the man and the woman have eaten the fruit, implying that sinfulness, like harmony, requires at least two interacting human beings. It is as if each discovered their own nakedness through the eyes of the other, as if nakedness reflected and refracted off another's response evoked the shame. Were they afraid to see themselves in God's eyes as well? Did they hide accordingly?

One cannot help but wonder what difference it might have made, had the couple, upon discovering nakedness, responded with joy, and run to God with the news of their discovery. Or, assuming shame was inevitable, what if the couple, rather than hiding from God, sought God out in repentance? In other words, wherein lies the knowledge of good and evil? Does knowing good and evil lie in the discovery of nakedness, in the subsequent shame, in covering the body, or in hiding from God in fear?[11] For the woman, the knowledge of good and evil makes childbirth painful, sex with her husband nevertheless still desirable, and subordination to the man inevitable. Thus reproduction, female sexual desire, and male power connect to generate both sexism and heterosexism. For the man this knowledge requires that throughout all his life he must labor with difficulty to till an unrelenting soil in order to have food to eat. In short, labor gets divided into reproductive and productive labor to establish gender difference in ways painful respectively for both the woman and the man. Power becomes sinfully skewed in favor of the man.

At this point Adam calls out his wife's name, Eve, in recognition that she is the mother of all living, as if the full implications of who she is in relation to a human future dawn on him for the first time. This dawning is fraught with ambiguity, for it affirms the future, a future that nevertheless privileges heterosexual males who successfully reproduce themselves. God then makes garments of skins to cover their nakedness and subsequently drives them from the garden, lest they learn the secret of eternal life.

As the only place where serious lines are drawn according to difference in gender, this part of the narrative is particularly important for what it does not say. First of all, the story does not ground reproduction in the stable household settings that we normally associate with family. The story says nothing about family life in itself at all. The text privileges reproduction and heterosexuality at a time when population guarantees the survival of the human species; nevertheless, the text does not mandate by divine decree that all subsequent human beings be heterosexual or that they necessarily reproduce. Pain in childbirth should not be confused with insisting that all women bear children in order to find fulfillment, nor with requiring that all pregnant women go full term. Though begetting is crucial to the human future at this point in human history, no particular sexual behavior or preference is universalized for all people in all times and places. The sexual and heterosexual connections of Eve to Adam through painful childbirth and desire, like Adam's rule over Eve, exemplify the consequences of sin, not the divine intention at the time of creation.

Furthermore, taken at face value, femininity and masculinity, as we normally think of them, are notable for their absence. The story focuses on nakedness, shame, covering the body, hiding from God in fear, bodily pain, a division of labor determined by sin, and an abuse of power. While the division of labor does depend on reproductive differences, there is no reference to a "weaker sex," associated with stereotypic femininity; on the contrary, Eve who mothers all who are living must be very strong to endure the pain of labor, as well as the subordination to Adam that she must suffer. Likewise, there is no reference to superiority of strength, intellect, spirit, or leadership, often stereotypically associated with masculinity; Adam may "rule" Eve, the content of which remains unspecified, but his rule is an abuse of power. Moreover, he himself becomes a slave to the earth for his livelihood. As one theologian has noted, rather than God authorizing specific gender differences accompanied by male supremacy, the text reads as if God were saying, "See what you've done! See what will follow from what you've done!" (Trible, 80).[12]

Only after Adam's recognition of the woman as Eve, the mother of all living, does God banish the couple, as if to say, "I cannot trust you now. If you stay here, you will probably eat from the tree of life. If you do so and learn how to live forever, there will be no relief from this awfulness; therefore, you must go from the garden."[13] For many Christians the subordination of women by men, a condition dependent on restricting character traits, tasks, and the distribution of power according to preconceived notions of gender, is quite simply sin. Likewise the privileging of hetero-sexuality. From this perspective, rather than divinely authorized, sexism and heterosexism are overridden by redemption, as proclaimed, for exam-ple, in Paul's letter to the Galatians, namely, that in Christ there is neither male nor female (3:28). The idea of restricting any virtue exclusively along the lines of gender and of constraining behavior according to sexual pref-erence reflects a fallen humanity rather than a redeemed one. Thus We-ber's restricting the traits associated with fatherhood solely to men is a mark of sin. By contrast, to extend virtues beyond their usual gendered restric-tions, as in the case of Miller-McLemore's extension of motherhood to in-clude all persons who care for others, is to proceed in light of redemption.

What makes gender difference an issue for family values is "rule." No matter how benign Weber's position on male domination in the home may be, he is still espousing women's subordination to men. Further-more, his position is moderate by comparison to others in the pro-family movement, as witnessed by the attacks of Pat Robertson, Marilyn Quayle, and others like them on feminism and on women who espouse reproductive choice and children's legal rights. Whereas Weber ad-dresses the issue of men abandoning their families, a phenomenon docu-mented by the small proportion of men who actually pay child support for their children, Robertson charges feminism as a movement that se-duces women into abandoning their children, or worse still, murdering them.[14] By abandoning children I take it Robertson means mothers en-tering the public work force; by murdering them I assume he means women choosing to abort fetuses. In neither case does he take into ac-count the possible circumstances which force such choices upon women. But even assuming that a woman enters the workforce out of a passion for her work or that she chooses to abort without guilt, simply because she does not want to be pregnant, she has not broken any law—a far cry from refusing to take court-ordered financial responsibility for one's children. One can only conclude here that the issue for Robertson, perhaps in con-trast to Weber, is power—getting it and keeping it—no matter at whose expense. Were Weber's viewpoint to become normative, women's free-dom would be seriously restricted; were Robertson's vision to become law, life for women would become unbearably cruel.

Thinking Difference

Comparing the various ways Genesis 2—3 gets interpreted, as well as comparing Weber's and Miller-McLemore's theological positions on gen-der and parenting, forces us to think about *how* we think difference, not only difference according to gender, but other differences crucial to understanding family life as well. As Christians we read scripture with the assumptions and values of the culture into which we are born. If that culture assumes and values hard-and-fast divisions along gender lines, then we will read accordingly. If the culture of our birth assumes a two-parent nuclear family as exclusively normative, then it does not matter whether ancient biblical families were polygamous and extended, or whether marriage was later viewed in the New Testament as a necessary evil to quell lust; we will read sacred texts as validation for two-parent, nuclear families. Unless we are willing to try to read scripture imaginatively from more than one perspective and to question our own norms in relation to what real families in our own culture look like, as well as how families are configured in other cultures, we can hardly read otherwise. Unless we can think difference differently, we cannot avoid doing serious damage to those people whose lives do not fulfill cultural expectations of what is normative.

What would it mean to think difference differently from within a Christian context? Thinking difference differently requires apprehending difference as the precursor to covenant rather than to conflict. Thinking difference differently means acknowledging that difference occurs within a wider context of relationship. Prior to human sinfulness, the narrative establishes a kinship among humans. This kinship entails a partnership among equals who are meant to stand side by side, related by their creatureliness to the earth, to other creatures, and to God as creator. Continuing in this vein, the Fall turns difference in relationship into ongoing division and conflict. Because the serpent and the humans defy God, the serpent is at odds with the humans, and the humans are at odds with God, one another, and the earth. Relationship, if it is to occur, can no longer occur innocently, but must overcome the condition that was intended to make relationship possible, namely, difference itself. How are humans to make the move from difference as division back to difference as the necessary possibility for harmonious relationship?

From a Christian perspective, in light of Jesus as Christ, God makes the first move, actually over and over again. God usually makes the first move by initiating a covenant, sometimes with a people (Exodus 35:1–19), sometimes written on the individual heart (Jeremiah 31:31), sometimes signified by bread and wine (Mark 14:22–25), but in any case, a covenant. These covenants generally emerge out of disasters or near disasters. These disasters and near disasters are often caused by human agency, as in the case of Cain's murdering Abel (Genesis 4:8), or are on occasion attributed to divine agency, as in the case of the plagues visited on the Egyptians (Exodus 7—13). God's sometimes questionable behavior notwithstanding, over and over again, so the biblical stories tell us, God seeks out relations with human creatures, sometimes by buying them back out of slavery—as in the redemption of the Israelites from Egypt (Exodus 14:1–30), sometimes by selling them back into slavery—as in the Babylonian captivity (Jeremiah 25).

These covenants characteristically focus on establishing right relations with God, among humans, and with the earth. Clearly from the divine perspective, these covenants are not between God and humans as if humans were equal to God. Furthermore, the covenants, expressed in human language, are contaminated by sexism, heterosexism, slavery, and ethnic prejudice within the human community. Nevertheless, whether made with Cain, Noah, Abraham, the Israelites, or the early followers of Jesus—whether marked on one's forehead (Genesis 4:15), carved on tablets of stone (Exodus 34:4), written on the human heart (Jeremiah 31:31), or sealed with the body and blood of Jesus (Mark 14:22–25)—the covenants carry within them an internal pressure toward human equality and harmonious relations among humans, harmony among all creatures, and harmony with God. The creation of the first humans as different but related foreshadows an ongoing process by which God works to overcome the continual human betrayal of relationship.

This betrayal manifests itself over and over again as an abuse of power justified in the name of false divisions, for which gender difference is only the first example given in the text. We perpetrate this betrayal wherever we rationalize economic, political, and social privilege in the name of divinely authorized differences. This kind of rationalization is no less true today when justifying on biblical grounds male privilege at the expense of women or heterosexual privilege at the expense of homosexual men and women, than it was in earlier times when Christians rationalized religious and racial privilege to justify the slaughter of Native Americans and the enslavement of Africans in this country. These same divisions according to race, class, gender, and sexual preference play themselves out today in Christian debate over family values. These divisions are overcome only when people repent and commit formally or informally with one another and with God to seek harmony together.

Repentance and commitment cannot take place, however, unless we understand the dynamics of how difference becomes the occasion for division. Division occurs when difference becomes the occasion for demonizing others, for masking their pain and suffering, and for stealing their futures. The way we normally conceive violence serves as a prime example of an interaction of demonizing others, their erasure or denial, and theft of the future that only further contributes to violence itself.

When we think of violence, we normally restrict it to the public arena by associating it with war and with crime in the streets. Both war and street violence depend for their perpetuation on a clearly designated dichotomy of allies and enemies. The enemy, rather than simply a human being with whom one disagrees, must become the demonized other for most of this kind of violence to take place. Largely as a result of our own ideologies of individualism, we tend further to restrict our conceptions of criminal violence to individual acts performed by one person on another, without wider reference to the violence done to many by our public institutions, ostensibly devoted to serving our citizenry. In some cases this ignorance of a wider context erases the victimization of those who suffer poverty because of exploitive business practices or lack of employment who may turn to crime, just as demonizing exaggerates their culpability. In other cases, if we are middle-class whites, we may have difficulties wrapping our minds around white-collar crime as a form of violence that steals the futures of others, for example, or we may further associate violence almost exclusively with males of color.

Furthermore, we neglect less visible forms of violence, in effect further erasing them from public view. Only recently, in no small part due to the women's movement, have we begun to include domestic battering, sexual abuse of both adults and children, and pornography, all of which we identify with the private realm, into our discourse on violence. Even now, we erase the pain and suffering of the victims of these privatized forms of violence because we still tend to imagine public forms of violence as definitive of the concept itself. Much of the concern for family values arises for liberals and conservatives alike in response to a perceived increase particularly in violence. This concern sometimes rests on questionable assumptions about the nature of violence and a simplistic classification of individuals as perpetrators and victims.

Demonizing the Other

For the Christian Coalition, for example, *violence* refers with very little exception almost exclusively to crime, particularly street crime related to gangs and drugs. By and large, militarism is confused with patriotism and not even recognized as participation in violence. The picture Reed presents in *Politically Incorrect,* for example, is one of good Christian people taking back the streets from the perpetrators whose acts threaten continued family existence and well-being (82ff.). The Christian Coalition, as well as the rest of us, should be concerned about street crime. It takes an especially heavy toll on families who live in poverty and in ghettos. Street crime, particularly gang-related crime, seriously disrupts neighborhoods;

drive-by shootings and gang rapes involve innocent bystanders as victims. In San Antonio, Texas, where I live, gang-related crime is one of the few forms of crime on the rise, and it is rising dramatically, particularly in the form of drive-by shootings. Most of the citizenry would agree that addressing this kind of violence, along with others, should be a top priority.

The question of how to address this kind of crime, however, generates conflicting responses that propose everything from curfews, punishing parents, and boot camps to gang summits. These proposals represent very different perspectives on authority and responsibility. Some of them, like curfews, are intended simply to contain the problem. Some proposals, like fining parents and sending juvenile offenders to boot camp, are simply punitive without reference to rehabilitation. Fining parents assumes that parents will subsequently take more control over disciplining their children. Sending juveniles and young adults to boot camp assumes that they will learn not to be violent, based on punishment. All these proposals share the assumption that gang members are other, "them" as opposed to "us." "They" are largely, though not exclusively, poor, young men and women of color. "We" are for the most part, though not entirely, Anglo-American, comparatively affluent men and women. "They" are largely urban dwellers who have begun to stray into the suburbs. "We" are largely suburbanites who fled the cities to escape their company to begin with.

By contrast, proposals like the gang summits organized by Wallis focus on involving offenders themselves in determining how to end their violence toward one another and toward everyone else. If connected with serious economic opportunity, the gang summits give people who are presently social and economic outsiders a stake in resolving conflict and creating positive, self-determined alternatives to life on the streets. By stressing that all gang members are brothers and sisters to one another, these summits focus on transcending narrowly defined conceptions of family and neighborhood that characterize gang thinking. Widening the concept *family* to include those who were previously enemies and rivals represents a radical alteration of consciousness for gang members.

These narrowly defined conceptions of family and neighborhood find their counterparts among affluent respectable citizens as well. Setting up the possibilities for a reconciliation among gangs across neighborhoods that extend in their effects throughout a city requires that adults committed to the well-being of the offenders share responsibility for helping to organize a summit. It further requires that affluent people commit to creating and sustaining viable economic opportunities that can compete with pushing drugs. For both of these things to happen, respectable citizens must think of gang members differently from how they normally think of them. Instead of problems to be controlled through punishment, gang members must become persons who need alternatives to their present situations. Instead of regarding gang members oppositionally as "them," gang members become part of "us."

In other words, in order for gang members to change, the people most threatened by them must change as well. Transformation among affluent citizens requires a shift in attitude from a fixation on taking back "our" streets from "them," to a commitment to figuring how to share the streets safely with everyone. Transformation must occur so that both parties cease to think in terms of "us and them." For gang members and respectable citizens alike, there must be a common commitment based on equality as persons, regardless of difference in power, status, age, class, race, ethnicity, and gender. Wallis sees this kind of commitment as central to the life of both urban and suburban churches and proposes active involvement of suburban churches with urban ones in promoting gang summits. While calling for this kind of change in attitude may strike some as idealistic, it appears to be working, in contrast to the more punitive proposals characteristically emerging from the pro-family movement, which so far appear to transform gang members into even more hardened criminals (Wallis, 16–20, 226–27, 241–42).

Erasing the Pain and Suffering of the Other

Gang-related violence represents only one form of violence, however. Moreover, it provides an easy target that lends itself well to political and ideological manipulation at election time. Violence occurs within the home as well as in the streets, and the pro-family movement, with very few exceptions, remains strangely silent on this matter. I picked Stu Weber's theology precisely because he is an exception to the rule on the issue of domestic battering. He at least considers it a problem for which men bear some responsibility. Nevertheless, for all his rejection of violence in the home, he does little to address the depth, range, and seriousness of the problem beyond simply urging men not to batter their wives. His position reflects little knowledge of the sociologies and pathologies of battering and sexual abuse. Worse still, many of his peers ignore the problems of domestic violence, at least in their public rhetoric. Reed, for example, sees divorce rather than violence in the home, as a primary exploitation of women. To reduce this form of exploitation, he proposes making divorce more difficult, a proposal that can only make escape from domestic violence more difficult for women than it already is (Reed, 258–59). Thus he erases from view violence toward women in the home.

Domestic abuse creates further complications for children, who as minors are not subject to full constitutional rights. Yet, the Christian Coalition endorses strengthening parental rights "to control the upbringing of their children" as one of the ten suggestions making up the *Contract with the American Family*.[15] Such legislation could curtail children's rights to safety, limit children's rights to sue their parents or to prosecute them for abuse, and require of adolescent females that they have parental consent for birth control or abortion. In homes where sexual abuse and battering are a way of life, strengthening parental control over the upbringing of children by limiting what little recourse is now legally available would only spell further disaster for them. Thus the Christian Coalition erases violence toward children within the home.

In addition, eliminating rather than expanding the rights of children in relation to their parents makes the Christian Coalition's stand against abortion ironic, to say the least. From the perspective of the pro-family movement, abortion constitutes violence toward an unborn child. The long-term goal of the pro-family movement is to end all legal rights to abortion, with the possible exception of when the mother's life is at risk. However, ending legal abortion will not only create more violence for women, forced as a consequence to seek illegal alternatives, but it will likely generate more violence toward children in the form of increased abuse against unwanted children. Guaranteeing the right to life for a fetus without reference to the circumstances by which it was conceived or into which it will be born, and further guaranteeing this right without respect for the safety and security of already-born adults and children, exhibits at best an ignorance of the nature of violence, and at worst an extraordinary hypocrisy. For many pregnant women who actually face the prospect of abortion, the decision of whether to abort or not is a tragic decision, fraught with moral ambiguity. The Christian Coalition's adamant, often effective, political opposition to women's right to make such a choice seems hardly in keeping with recognizing the image of God within the women faced by such a choice. This opposition becomes especially cruel in its effects on poor women who have no recourse other than Medicaid.

Violence within the family is not confined to the abuse of spouses and children, but is directed toward the elderly of both genders as well. Neither religious conservatives nor liberals have taken on the issue of the abuse of older adults by family members and some of the institutions outside the home responsible for their care. For families headed by adults working outside the home, whether they are affluent or among the working poor, caring for elderly family members can create a living hell that may degenerate quickly into abuse. Nevertheless, the Christian Coalition has fought relentlessly and successfully to defeat universal health care, and liberals have yet even to awaken to the problems faced by abused and abusers alike. Thus violence toward the elderly disappears as an issue confronting public consciousness.

The Christian Coalition's deafening silence on the issue of violence within the family casts its stand against pornography, yet another form of violence, in an ambiguous light as well. Reed, for example, views pornography as another primary form of exploitation of women and children, and many feminists would concur. This view is further reflected in the *Contract with the American Family*, which includes as one of its ten suggestions a proposal to enact legislation against pornography in a variety of forms. The Contract specifies laws to keep pornography off the Internet, to make it easier for parents to block programs on cable television, and to make possession of child pornography illegal.

In regard to policing the Internet, software that can block pornography already exists, though this software is incapable of blocking on-line conversation. With the exception of technological devices making it easier for parents to block programs on cable television, the issue of restricting pornography in any form beyond snuff films and child pornography, both of which are covered by other laws, generates the usual constitutional conflicts. These include the problem of defining *obscenity;* the difficulty of distinguishing pornography from erotica; the potential for violating First Amendment guarantees to free speech, particularly with respect to censoring artistic creation and journalistic speech; the controversy over whether pornography causes or reflects violence; the controversy over whether the consumption of pornography is strictly a matter of privacy or a public issue; the controversy over whether adult performers are consenting adults or forced labor; and the problems that arise from trying to distinguish legally between hard-core and soft-core pornography.

In regard to the pro-family movement, its stand against pornography arises from a wider context that includes strong support for male-dominated families, a long history of homophobia, and highly selective attacks on the film industry. This should give the rest of us who find pornography deeply disturbing and repulsive on other grounds serious pause before deciding to cast our lot with the pro-family movement on this issue. Nevertheless, we should also understand that silence on the issue is itself a form of erasure that colludes with the violence of pornography.

Stealing the Future of the Other

Last but not least, beyond both public crime and domestic abuse, violence includes ecological violence. Throughout the theological spectrum from left to right, with very few exceptions, Christians have not considered care for the earth as a specifically *family* value. Ecologically committed Christians have been slow to connect care for the earth as a human responsibility in general to the rights and responsibilities of particular families, though Christians concerned with ecofeminism and ecojustice have connected violation of the environment to other forms of violence perpetrated among human beings.[16] The pro-family movement has consistently aligned itself with legislative efforts to deregulate government, including environmental deregulation. Its earlier more apocalyptic stance during the '70s and '80s that justified nuclear holocaust and ecological devastation as biblical signs of an impending rapture made repairing environmental damage and sustaining life across species on this planet irrelevant.[17] Yet, that we can even consider a future for our children and grandchildren without reference to any commitment to a reduction in waste, to clean air and water, to uncontaminated soil, and to a climate that can sustain ecological diversity is incomprehensible. Ceasing to ravage the earth is a necessary condition to the existence of families in the future; however, care for the earth as a family value has yet to appear on the table for discussion.

Conclusion

Thinking difference differently requires acknowledging how we warp difference into division among us: by demonizing one another, by erasing the pain and suffering of one another, by stealing the future from us all. Both Wallis and Reed are right in calling for a transformation of the heart, though they obviously have very different kinds of transformation in mind. For such a transformation to occur we must learn to imagine better. We must not forget that Cain, who is an outcast, is our brother, that Tamar, who disappears, is our sister, and that the earth, created good, is in our care for generations not yet begotten. The damage to family life wrought by violence far and away exceeds the imaginations of those who number themselves among both the religious left and the religious right. Christians across the spectrum of theological and political perspectives need to expand their conceptions of both the breadth and the depth of the violence that characterizes family life. Violence in its many permutations renders present family life miserable for many, and it threatens to destroy the future for all.

The problems posed by violence are monumental in scope and cannot be solved quickly or easily. Addressing them requires a spiritual disciplining of the imagination that results in acting both locally and partially from within a more global network. For networks to form and action to occur, however, covenants must be critically renewed and in some cases new covenants must be made. Christians in the United States belong to long-standing political traditions of making covenants. We have focused for the most part on religious traditions so far. It is time now to turn to our political traditions as resources as well. They too require of us that we think difference differently.

Creation in the image of God places human-divine relationship at the center of human identity, superseding all other relations including particular family and religious relations. That God created *all* humans in God's image establishes a kinship among humans that forms one of the two necessary conditions for all particular human relationships, namely, commonality. That God created humans different from one another, as witnessed by the creation of Adam and Eve, constitutes the second necessary condition for all particular human relationships.

Sin is the warping of difference into division based on skewed power, exemplified in Adam's rule over Eve. The warping of difference into division extends far beyond gender, however, to include racial, ethnic, class, age, and creedal differences as well. Its effects are felt today in the violence that permeates family life. By contrast, redemption symbolizes God's ongoing work, from the earliest covenants to the present, to repair and reconcile human relations with God and with one another.

Through Jesus the Christ, we as Christians acknowledge that God's repair and reconciliation have begun their work in our lives. We are participants in a covenant that does not supersede God's work of redemption signified by earlier covenants, but does extend the knowledge of redemption even to the Gentiles. As Christians we are thus called to distinguish differences among us from division based on false rule and to celebrate differences, including religious differences, among human creatures as gifts of God.

Our faith requires that our loyalty to our own particular families and faiths signifies ever-widening loyalties—to the human family as the people of God, to the earth from which we are created, and to God who created us as equal to one another, but different in a multitude of ways. Freedom to celebrate in the midst of ever-expanding loyalties arises for Christians from trusting that we are not our own; we are God's. Belonging to God frees us to love this finite order, including one another as ourselves, as God's creation, according to the covenants we make with God and with one another.

Within this finite order, our religious freedom lies in the liberty to worship the God to whom we belong without interference from the government, even when we ourselves are the government. This freedom that comes from belonging to God allows us to enter into political activity aimed to effect radical democracy as equal partners with vastly different people, bound to one another by continually evolving covenantal relations. How then do we resolve conflicts generated by division within this context of making covenants? What does the freedom of belonging to God have to do with how we exercise political choice and responsibility?

Part 2

Created for Covenant

4

The Moment of Silence

The U.S. Constitution, as it continues to evolve, reflects multiple views of freedom. The document emerged historically out of both Christian theological traditions and modern philosophical traditions. These traditions have sometimes stood at odds with each other on the origin and end of human freedom itself, as well as on the nature of ultimate authority. These contending views of freedom emerged historically from conflicting religious, political, and economic interests that continue into the present. Nevertheless, a religious tradition of covenant making and a political tradition that emphasized the natural rights of individuals, bound to mutual protection by the social contract, joined together to produce the law of the land. Though the Constitution is not a covenant made between God and humans, it is a covenant made among humans, to form a country out of a revolution declared in the name of the "laws of Nature and Nature's God."[1]

Those who wrote the Constitution did so with the idea in mind of changing it to accommodate changing times. They set up a system of checks and balances among the legislative, judicial, and executive branches of government, and they established procedures to amend the Constitution in the future, though they deliberately made amending the Constitution difficult in order to avoid triviality. In over two hundred years, this country has legislated only twenty-seven amendments, two of which repeal previous amendments.

The present Congress is considering proposing two amendments that set limitations on the rights and responsibilities guaranteed under the First Amendment in the Bill of Rights. The first amendment would prohibit desecrating the American flag, a constraint on free speech. The second amendment purports to protect the religious liberties of Americans in public places, a constraint on the prohibition against establishing a state religion. In addition, Congress continues to consider amendments to ban abortion, to allow organized prayer in the public schools, and to require a balanced federal budget.

Many Christians, particularly members of the Christian Coalition, strongly support all of these amendments, as well as additional similar legislation proposed in the *Contract with the American Family*. They support this legislation on the grounds that it directly or indirectly represents mainstream family values of patriotism, religious observance, the protection of unborn children, the rejection of secular humanism, and an end to big government. Earlier chapters have addressed how detrimental it is to family life and to justice from a Christian perspective to think of culture in terms of mainstream and margin. This chapter and chapter 5 focus on the theological implications of some of this legislation for constitutional rights to religious freedom.

The Constitution as Covenant

Given that the Constitution emerged in part from a theological tradition of covenant making, Christians face several questions concerning our relation to the Constitution. Can the way Christians think about covenant relations with God provide guidelines for how Christians think about the Constitution? How might we as citizens assess conflicts over constitutional rights? Can we find resolution to these conflicts without further amending the Constitution? What are the political, social, religious, and theological implications of the additional legislation suggested by the Christian Coalition's *Contract with the American Family*? For Christians who disagree with the Christian Coalition's agenda what are the theological and political alternatives?

While raising these questions, I shall argue that covenant relations with God require of Christians that they discern carefully the difference between the finiteness of their values and the infinite source of all finite values. To mistake the finite as infinite is to commit idolatry. Covenant relations with God further require that Christians, in their political deliberations, give priority to protecting society's most vulnerable citizens and addressing their suffering; this is no small part of what mutual respect among all humans is about. While they cannot by themselves resolve all conflicts, these convictions of faith provide guidelines that aid in deciding conflicts in constitutional rights and in extending these rights to currently unprotected groups. These guidelines further aid in determining to what extent the Constitution needs to be modified, to what extent the additional legislation proposed by the Christian Coalition actually enhances family life, and what possible alternatives may exist in the way of action taken by Christians in behalf of political reform.

To clarify what is at stake in the legislation currently proposed in light of a history of covenant making, I shall pose a series of dilemmas. This chapter deals with the issue of religious observance in the public schools; chapter 5 addresses problems raised by government intervention into family life on behalf of minor children in a religious context. Whereas mandated religious observance in the public schools raises the issue of idolatry, state intervention into family life raises issues of justice toward those least able to assume responsibility for their own lives.

In regard to religious expression in the public schools, the issue is usually posed as a conflict of one's free exercise of religious beliefs with the establishment of a state religion, and this conflict is indeed central to understanding the issue. At the same time, we practice a civil religion in this country, exemplified by the swearing of oaths on the witness stand, the pledge of allegiance said daily in public schools, the marking of money in the name of God, and the ceremonial swearing in of elected officials. Are not all of these occasions infringements on the First Amendment rights of nonbelievers and those whose religious faiths are not monotheistic? Or does the context of the mandatory public education of minors make a difference? Does even a voluntary but publicly specified moment of silence arguably constitute a state infringement on the rights of children to free exercise? Last but not least, do public religious observances in the public schools infringe on parents' rights to raise their children according to their own family values, whether these values are religious or opposed to religious practices and beliefs?

The Priority of God

God continually seeks to redeem human life from sin by initiating covenants with the people of God. These covenants are partial in the sense that no single one of them addresses the full particularities of all circumstances for all humans beings for all times. They nevertheless set the boundaries for right relations with God and with others. In particular, in regard to right relations with God, the covenant made at Sinai establishes the priority of God in human life. Initially carved in stone and presented before a community (Exodus 24:12), this covenant is likewise to be written on the human heart (Jeremiah 31:31). According to this covenant, as well as later ones, God's priority in human life manifests itself most especially in two forms.

First, there shall be no other gods before the God of creation and redemption; thus the people of God are prohibited from committing idolatry (Exodus 20:2–3). The prohibition against idolatry extends beyond the making of finite objects like golden calves and bowing down to them in false worship, to include as well the elevation of any finite value to the status of infinite worth or value. According to theologians from Augustine to Martin Luther to H. Richard Niebuhr to Paul Tillich, that which consumes one's heart is her god, whether it be work, particular other people, family life, loyalty to one's nation, or loyalty to one's particular religious traditions.[2] Thus God must take priority over everything and everyone we hold dear. The priority of God does not make that which is finite worthless; rather it clarifies the source of all worth, thereby placing the finite within a wider perspective. All that God has made possesses positive worth by virtue of being God's creation.

Second, for God to be central and prior to all other loyalties in human life, humans must seek justice in relation to one another and in their treatment of the earth. As Christians we share with Jews and Muslims God's requirement to do justice, to love kindness, and to walk humbly with God (Micah 6:8). Jesus calls us specifically as Christians to feed the hungry, give drink to the thirsty, welcome the stranger, clothe the naked, visit the sick, and go to those in prison (Matthew 25:36). Christians conventionally interpret such passages to mean that, if we do good things for people in dire circumstances, we are Christlike and worthy of admission into heaven. Frankly, such an interpretation assumes self-interest as a primary motivation and rests on fairly middle-class assumptions that individual acts of charity either reflect faith or promote merit. To my mind, these texts and others like them mean something far more radical, namely, that God is to be found first and foremost with the outcast. Rather than making us Christlike, doing justice permits us to discover the image of God in the face of the other, the stranger, the enemy, the reject, the untouchable. This image, through no effort on our part, redeems us by allowing us to recognize the image of God within ourselves. God delivers us from sin by calling us to where God is, and, when it comes to justice, God, according to scripture, is first and foremost with the suffering and afflicted. This identification of God with what is not normative, not at the center of power, not mainstream, and not conventionally acceptable puts the pressure on all covenants to exceed their partiality.

The prohibition against idolatry and the mandate to seek justice, while they may not resolve all dilemmas, nevertheless provide critical guidelines for assessing the political conflicts over family values within which we find ourselves presently embroiled.

Constitutional Priorities

The Constitution of the United States, like any other covenant, is a partial covenant; that is, it is located in a particular history. The document originally rests on certain assumptions that we today would find narrow and oppressive. For example, slavery was legal, and slaves were property rather than persons in any legal sense. Women and children of all races, ethnicities, and classes were likewise property. Only adult, white males who held property could vote; thus, poor white males, slaves, and women and children of all races, ethnicities, and classes were excluded from full participation in the new democracy. Thus the Constitution restricted the equality of all men to a certain class of predominantly Anglo-European males, viewed as free, autonomous individuals entering voluntarily into a compact with one another. Furthermore, the compact worked to sustain their economic, racial, and gender privilege as a compact among states not to infringe on the free trade of money.[3]

The Bill of Rights itself reflects the limitations of the original document. Almost before the ink had dried on the page, the Constitution needed amending. The first ten amendments were added to specify and protect the rights of the new citizens. Nevertheless, they too manifest problematic assumptions about what it means to be human, to be equal, and to live "with liberty and justice for all." For example, the Bill of Rights assumes the affluence of those eligible to vote as given and therefore makes no provision for food, shelter, nurture, education, health care, and work. There is no acknowledgment that the men, rather than autonomous, were dependent on the forced labor of others for the very necessities that made their adulthood, their affluence, and their citizenship possible. The subsequent history of the United States of America could be written in part as a struggle to address and redress these limitations ever since.

Serious limitations notwithstanding, the early founders who produced the document did much that deserves praise. The Constitution as amended creates a democracy based on the consent of the governed. The governed themselves consent not only to representative rule that is of, for, and by the people, they also consent to a rule of law. There are two remarkable features to this rule of law. First, the law contains within it procedures by which the law, including the Constitution itself, can be modified. Building in the ability to change has thus allowed the extension of fundamental rights to previously excluded groups. Second, the content of the law emphatically protects the right to dissent. The early founders considered this right so fundamental that it appears as the First Amendment, the first article in the Bill of Rights. The constitutional freedoms—free speech, freedom to assemble, freedom to petition the government, freedom of the press, and freedom of religion—as further reinforced by the Fourteenth Amendment, assure that citizens may nonviolently disagree with their own government at all levels without fear of punishment. As we struggle with our own political and spiritual crises, as we today confront the need for change, we must keep in mind that our citizenship requires consent to law, a law that protects dissent. We are not citizens of a democracy determined solely by the will of a voting majority at any given point in time.

The significance of exercising the right to dissent is crucial to understanding present conflicts over religious expression and public religious observance. People jailed or denied political rights for their religious and political convictions numbered heavily among those who established the colonies. The leaders of the revolution against England, who went on to lead the newly formed country, included not only religious dissidents but also atheists and free thinkers. The dissent of a minority in the face of the majority played a crucial role in ending slavery, extending the vote to women, and struggling for civil rights for African Americans. Thus, guaranteeing the right to dissent not only protects those who actively voice their disagreement but can protect those minorities yet to be heard. Exercising the right to dissent reinforces the possibility that the most helpless and least powerful members of this society may seek and find justice.

Amending the Constitution to mandate prayer in the public schools, along with other legislation currently proposed or supported by the Christian Coalition, threatens the right to dissent. In order to understand the nature of this threat, we must first examine briefly the history of Supreme Court involvement with religious expression, observance, and practice, with a particular focus on the Court's involvements with the public schools.

The First Amendment states, "Congress shall make no law respecting an establishment of religion, or prohibiting the free exercise thereof."[4] The first clause has come to be known as the "establishment clause;" the second clause is commonly referred to as the "free exercise clause." The two, taken together, create what Thomas Jefferson described as "a wall of separation" between church and state, now more commonly interpreted as the separation of religion and state.[5]

The separation of religion and state was first tested in *Reynolds v.*

United States (1878), which addressed whether the state may make secular laws that supersede free exercise, in this instance, a law against bigamy. George Reynolds, a Mormon, faced a $500 fine and five years' imprisonment for bigamy. The defense claimed that his church required this practice and that his refusal would result in his eternal damnation. The Court ruled against Reynolds on behalf of the right of the state to establish laws overriding religious practices on behalf of a public interest that is secular in origin.[6]

Since this time, a number of judicial conflicts have arisen in regard to the separation of religion and state. These conflicts have involved a range of issues, including whether people opposed to swearing oaths on religious grounds are exempt from taking oaths in court or swearing allegiance to the flag, whether Native Americans who practice peyote rituals as a matter of faith are in violation of drug laws, whether religious symbols may be erected on government property, whether state legislatures may open daily sessions with prayer, whether the state may fund private religious education in any form, whether people may remove their underage children from public education on religious grounds, whether zoning laws may be established to prevent the religious sacrifice of animals, whether specified time for prayer, meditation, or a moment of silence can be set aside during the school day in public schools, and whether the state may intervene in the religious upbringing of children for the purpose of requiring medical treatment. We shall focus here on religious observance in the public schools and on state intervention on behalf of children.

Religious Observance in the Public Schools

Some Christians perceive the Court's prohibition of prayer in the public schools as a conflict between the free exercise of religion and the state's establishment of a religion. In *Politically Incorrect*, Reed, for example, has formulated the issue of public religious observance largely by emphasizing free exercise and by attempting to refute the claim that religious expression in public places constitutes a state establishment of religion (75–78). The issue is far more complicated, however. As we shall see, some religious observances in public places, like organized prayer in the public schools and including a moment of silence, not only violate the prohibition against a state establishment of religion, but also promote the free exercise of religion by some at the expense of the free exercise of religion by others as well.

In *Engel v. Vitale* (1962), the Supreme Court ruled that required prayer in the public schools violated the establishment clause of the First Amendment. At issue was a brief, monotheistic but nondenominational prayer, written by the New York State Board of Regents and required daily in the public schools. Among those opposed to the prayer were devoutly religious people offended by its generic nature. Among other things, the definition of what constitutes government establishment was at issue. The Court distinguished between explicit conscious intent on the part of the state and indirect effect. In regard to free exercise of religion, plaintiffs had to prove that government intent to prohibit was explicit. In regard to state establishment of religion, the plaintiffs needed only to show that establishment was the effect of a government activity. The Court ruled that mandated prayer in the public schools had the effect of establishing state religion. In defense of his opposition to organized school prayer, Justice Hugo L. Black wrote:

> The Establishment Clause, unlike the Free Exercise Clause, does not depend upon any showing of direct governmental compulsion and is violated by the enactment of laws which establish an official religion, whether those laws operate directly to coerce non-observing individuals or not. . . . [The clause] stands as an expression of principle on the part of the Founders of our Constitution that religion is too personal, too sacred, too holy, to permit its "unhallowed perversion" by a civil magistrate.[7]

In other words, Black ruled that organized school prayer effectively established a state religion.

In 1970 the Supreme Court ruled against Pennsylvania's statutory program to reimburse private religious schools for secular educational services in *Lemon v. Kurtzman*. At this time the Court established what came to be known as the "Lemon test" for deciding cases involving freedom of religion. The Lemon test involves three criteria: First, state legislation must be for a secular purpose. Second, the effect of the legislation must neither advance nor prohibit religion. Third, legislation must neither foster excessive governmental entanglement with religion nor create an excessive degree of political division along religious lines.[8] The Lemon test has continued to play a major role in determining Court decisions on relations between religion and state, including the issues of organized school prayer and mandated moments of silence.

Both *Engel v. Vitale* and *Lemon v. Kurtzman* were landmark decisions. *Engel v. Vitale* in particular created a furor, once it was enforced in the public schools. The response to *Engel v. Vitale* on the part of several state legislatures was to enact legislation mandating a moment of silence during which students might voluntarily pray, meditate, contemplate, or introspect. In *Wallace v. Jaffee* (1985) the Court struck down an Alabama statute mandating just such a moment. The Court not only reaffirmed *Engel v. Vitale* and *Lemon v. Kurtzman*, but extended prohibition against school prayer to include a required moment of silence during which students might voluntarily pray.

It is important to point out what did not get prohibited at this time, or at any time since the initial ruling. At no time has the Court prohibited voluntary individual prayer in the public schools, provided that such prayers were not conducted in a disruptive manner. Quite the contrary, in *Tinker v. Des Moines Independent School District* (1969), the Court ruled that "it can hardly be argued that either students or teachers shed their constitutional rights to freedom of speech or expression at the schoolhouse gate."[9] At issue from a purely legal perspective are the level of state involvement and the extent to which moments of silence are themselves religious practices that advance or prohibit particular traditions. The education of minors is mandatory; for children who cannot afford private religious education, public schools are the only alternative. From a judicial perspective, whether a spoken prayer or a moment of silence, such practices violate not only the establishment clause but the free exercise clause as well. Furthermore, minor children attending public schools are in the care of parents who may or may not be religious, and if religious, represent increasingly diverse traditions. To require particular religious observances that conflict with the practices and teachings in the home constitutes an illegal and unnecessary intervention of the state into family life. *May v. Cooperman* (1983), tried in the New Jersey federal court, illustrates well the problems involved even in an organized moment of silence.

In March 1982, fifty-five members of the New Jersey legislature introduced statute 1064 directing principals and teachers in every public school in New Jersey to set aside a one-minute period of silence for voluntary private "contemplation and introspection."[10] The bill was passed over the governor's veto and went into effect on December 16, 1982. On January 10, 1983, an action was filed against the New Jersey Board of Education and the New Jersey legislature, seeking that the statute be declared unconstitutional.. The presiding judge granted an injunction temporarily restraining implementation of the statute. The trial began on September 13, 1983, and the judge ruled in favor of the plaintiffs on October 24, 1983, though he denied them restitution for court costs.

Plaintiffs included Jeffrey May, a teacher who refused to conduct the moment of silence on the grounds that it was a religious observance and who was subsequently threatened by his superiors with disciplinary action, and children and their parents, some of whom were not religious and some of whom were Catholic and Jewish. The nonreligious plaintiffs objected on the grounds that the moment of silence was an enforced religious observance, and therefore, the state establishment of religion. The religious plaintiffs objected on the additional grounds that they were opposed to this particular religious observance as an infringement on their rights of free exercise. The defendants included Dr. Saul Cooperman, New Jersey Commissioner of the New Jersey Department of Education, charged with the implementation of the statute, along with various local boards of education and the New Jersey legislature. The defendants argued that the moment of silence was not specifically religious and was intended as a moment of transition from home life to school life. They argued further that, as a ritual of transition, the moment of silence had pedagogical value by setting boundaries between what went on outside the classroom and what went on inside it.

The plaintiffs presented several kinds of evidence that the moment of silence was a religious observance. This evidence included the history of the bill and its predecessors, expert testimony on the lack of educational value of such a practice, the treatment by school officials of students who refused to observe the moment of silence, and expert testimony defining religion and religious observance. Regarding the history of the bill, the plaintiffs argued that the legislature's intent for the moment of silence was clearly religious on the grounds that members of the New Jersey legislature had justified the bill during legislative hearings by appeal to religious reasons. So, for example, when one legislator asked another why such a bill was necessary, he answered that students would not pray publicly unless so directed. The lawyers for the plaintiffs also called educational experts who testified that there was no academic or pedagogical merit for such a moment. In addition to questionable intent and lack of educational value, the plaintiffs further argued that, for those who refused to observe silence, the effects had been punitive and emotionally damaging. In regard to punitive consequences, one of the plaintiffs, a high school student, requested that he be allowed to leave the room. His teacher sent him to the school office for a determination, but on his way there, the student was stopped by a teacher who insisted that the student immediately observe the silence. The student refused, claiming that it was enforced prayer, upon which refusal he was charged with insubordination and suspended. In regard to emotional damage, a Jewish couple asked their young child not to participate in the moment of silence on religious grounds and to request to leave the room instead. The child became so upset at the thought of being singled out and separated from the other children that the parents withdrew their request. In another instance, Catholic parents objected to a moment of silence on the grounds that it was an invasion of their responsibilities as parents for the religious upbringing of their two daughters; they, nevertheless, did not instruct their daughters to leave the room because they wished to avoid putting their daughters in an embarrassing situation in regard to the rest of their peers.

Last but not least, the plaintiffs presented expert testimony regarding the nature of religion and religious observance to argue that a moment of silence was a religious rather than a secular observance. Langdon Gilkey, then professor of theology at the University of Chicago Divinity School, testified that religious observance, notably through ritual practices of prayer and participation in the sacraments, was central to the definition of religion and religious faith. He testified that prayer to God took different forms for the different monotheistic traditions, and that for nontheistic traditions like Buddhism, adherents observed meditation rather than prayer. He further pointed out that among all the different traditions, prayer and meditation took a variety of forms, including standing, kneeling, kneeling on a prayer rug, sitting, bowing one's head, looking up, closing one's eyes, leaving the eyes open, vocalizing, chanting, and remaining silent.

As Gilkey explained, an organized moment of silence, even where prayer is voluntary and meditation an option, mandates a particular form of prayer, simultaneously excluding other postures and other forms of religious expression. So, for example, even though one need not pray during the moment of silence, one could not pray a traditional Muslim prayer, which is vocalized while kneeling on a prayer rug, or perform a traditional Hindu or Buddhist meditation involving a chant. Nor could an Orthodox Jew pray aloud with arms outstretched or a Catholic kneel while crossing herself. In other words, the practice of a moment of silence, performed whether standing or sitting, is in fact a specifically Protestant religious observation. Enforced silence thus prohibits the free exercise of religion on the part of those whose traditions differ from Protestant traditions. Rev. George D. Younger, representing the American Baptist Churches of New Jersey, further testified that enforced religious observance might induce cynicism and the rejection of religion, with which Gilkey concurred.

The defendants presented comparatively and substantively little evidence on behalf of their case. They argued that the moment of silence had a secular purpose which was to mark a period of transition. Dr. Adam Scrupski, an associate professor of the Rutgers Graduate School of Education, testified that such moments served the pedagogical function of establishing or reinforcing the boundary between school and the outside world. Dr. Stanley L. Rosner, professor of the College of Education of Temple University, offered countertestimony on behalf of the plaintiffs that there was no evidence that any school in New Jersey was having difficulty with transitions from the outside world to the classroom. The plaintiffs further pointed out that, in any case, reciting the pledge of allegiance, a common practice throughout the state school systems, marked a distinctive transition. The defendants also offered evidence from the Sayreville public schools, where the practice had been employed since the Supreme Court had rejected organized school prayer in 1969, that the moment of silence did no damage to students and was met with no objection by students or parents. The plaintiffs offered as counterevidence the Princeton public schools, a much more religiously diverse school district, where there was strong resistance from both students and parents.

Upon considering the evidence presented by both sides, the judge ruled for the plaintiffs on several grounds. Not only did he find the evidence presented by the plaintiffs more compelling, but he found that the evidence presented by the defense failed to meet the criteria of the Lemon test. He ruled that Bill 1604 had no secular purpose on two counts: The legislative process by which the bill was enacted indicated that the intent of its sponsors was religious. In addition, Dr. Scrupski, the expert witness who claimed that the moment of silence had educational value, simply could not under scrutiny substantiate the claim; furthermore, he had been brought into the case long after the bill had become law, indicating to the judge that legislative concern for a secular purpose was after the fact, rather than part of the intent. Thus Bill 1604 failed the first criterion of the Lemon test.

The judge also found that, in violation of the second criterion of the Lemon test, Bill 1604 both advanced and prohibited religion. The judge found that the posture required of students during the moment of silence advanced Protestant practices; he further noted that, as a particular religious observance, it inhibited religion by virtue of being mandatory rather than voluntary. In regard to this point the judge distinguished moments of silence in the public schools from the practices of civil religion by arguing that civil religious practices are ceremonial functions that do not have the effect of establishing a religion because they are not necessarily responses of a believer to an ultimate reality. He went on to add that mandating a moment of silence prevented other forms of prayer and moreover disregarded the beliefs of the nonreligious and the antireligious. Besides failing to meet the first two criteria of the Lemon test, Bill

1604 violated the third stipulation as well; the judge found that a mandated moment of silence promoted excessive divisiveness among and between religious groups as witnessed by the testimony of the plaintiffs regarding the effects on their children and as witnessed by the experience of parents and children in the Princeton public schools.

The judge's rationale for the decision of *May v. Cooperman* obviously reveals the judge's concern to prevent the establishment of religion by the state. More important, the judge's reasoning in this particular case demonstrates a clear and consistent concern to protect the free exercise of religion as well. At no time does he attack religious expression; rather his point is that the free expression or exercise of religion must be just that—free. Free exercise cannot be mandated, nor can one group's practices be privileged over others. This conscientious concern to protect the rights established by both clauses of the First Amendment freedom of religion typically characterizes the decisions handed down by the courts.[11]

The Religious Liberties Amendment

The first Supreme Court ruling against mandated school prayer has nevertheless produced no small confusion regarding what can and cannot happen in the classroom and in the public square in regard to religious practice. Furthermore, in some of its rulings on free exercise cases, the Court has exhibited bias in favor of Protestant assumptions and conceptions of religion.[12] The Christian Coalition's concern to protect the exercise of religious liberties in public places emerges partly out of this confusion, though also as an attempt to assert its own values as dominant in the culture. In the *Contract with the American Family*, the Coalition proposes a constitutional amendment that would allow "voluntary, student and citizen-initiated free speech in non-compulsory settings such as courthouse lawns, high school graduation ceremonies, and sports events."[13] Such a proposal is unnecessary because no authority prohibits individual free exercise and because the exercise of civil religion in public places is legally protected. The proposal is moreover a threat to both clauses of the First Amendment freedom of religion. If enacted, such a proposal only further confuses the issue of public religious observance. Worse still, it potentially fosters division within religious groups, among religious groups, and between religious and nonreligious people. There are other, better alternatives than the proposal for such an amendment.

Such an amendment is unnecessary because free speech is already guaranteed by the First Amendment, and religious expression is protected by free speech unless and until religious expression constitutes a state establishment of religion or prohibits the free exercise of religion. Moreover, recurring court struggles with what kinds of religious expression are appropriate in the public square are struggles that should be ongoing rather than truncated. In addition to First Amendment guarantees, the interaction of the legislative, judicial, and executive branches protects dissent. This dissent implicitly manifests itself today in part through increasing religious diversity. Not only does the proposal fail to address this diversity, but it also obstructs the central processes designed to protect such diversity.

In addition to being unnecessary, the proposal is coercive. As such it violates both the establishment clause and the free exercise clause stated in the First Amendment.

In regard to the establishment clause, there are several problems. People already have the right to pray publicly on all kinds of ceremonial occasions, as witnessed by the observances of civil religion. Elected officials swear oaths of office in the name of God. Chaplains open legislative sessions with prayer. Nevertheless, public education differs from the contexts in which civil religion is practiced. Public attendance at most events where civil religion is observed is voluntary. By contrast the law requires that children receive an education until a certain age (usually sixteen), and the public schools provide the primary means by which this law is upheld. Furthermore, while events like graduation and sports events are themselves voluntary in a technical sense, children should not be denied access to such celebrations in order to avoid religious coercion, however unintended.[14] The proposal calls for legitimating voluntary acts that constitute organized, regular, formal events, occurring in the context of public education, whether civil religious observances or observances of a particular religious tradition. By virtue of their formality, they are mandated unofficially, if not officially.

If public events like graduation from high school and athletic events begin with a student-or citizen-initiated prayer for which all members of an audience are asked to bow their heads, for whom is the exercise voluntary? Perhaps for those who initiate the observance, but what about the rest of the audience? What if atheists wish to shout during such a moment? Will Hindus be allowed simultaneously to initiate prayer, or Wiccans be allowed to dance? Publicly exhorting an audience to prayer in the context of public education, no matter what kind of prayer and however voluntarily initiated, has the effect of coercion. To observe civil religion or any other kind in this context violates the establishment clause because such an observance would be by default mandatory. The proposal as it stands lends itself easily to a state establishment of religion by effect, even if not by intention.

In addition to violating the establishment clause, the proposal threatens to erode the right to free exercise. If legislated in any form, the proposal would erode the free exercise clause by advancing one religion in ways that prohibit others, unless, of course, the Christian Coalition is willing to allow students and citizens to initiate chanting and dancing, among other possible practices, as part of graduation ceremonies, sports events, and other similar ceremonies.

Besides being unnecessary and coercive, the proposal potentially promotes division along religious lines and between religious and nonreligious groups and individuals. The chief rationale for the proposal rests on the claim that public institutions are hostile toward religious people and that evangelicals and fundamentalists in particular are, as a group, the object of extreme bigotry, not unlike the bigotry experienced by African Americans at the expense of white racists (Reed, 41–51). The text explaining the proposal claims a loss of religious rights because of court intervention. In fact, as we have just seen in the decision on *May v. Cooperman*, what is lost is the right to impose one's religious beliefs on others. Religious people may still pray in public, whether Christian or otherwise. Christians can and do run for political office and get elected in large numbers. Evangelical Protestants in particular have been highly successful at getting elected to political office, most notably Jimmy Carter and Mark Hatfield. This claim of religious bigotry is ironic, given how difficult it would be (if not impossible) for any politician to get elected to office in this country without professing some form of specifically Christian faith.

Such a claim would be laughable, were it not so divisive. Reed speaks of institutional hostility toward people of faith while exonerating the anti-Semitic, racist, sexist, and homophobic polemical excesses of his own president, Pat Robertson. Though Reed makes overtures toward religiously conservative African Americans, Catholics, and Jews by acknowledging past excesses on the part of his religious brethren, at no time throughout *Politically Incorrect* does he include Muslims or any non-monotheistic religious groups in the people of faith when arguing for religious dialogue and coalition. Needless to say, from Reed's perspective atheists and agnostics are part of the problem rather than the solution.

Conclusion

There are other alternatives to such an unnecessary, coercive, divisive constitutional amendment, as well as any other amendment that espouses any form of mandated prayer in the public schools. For example, we need clarification regarding what Supreme Court decisions on public

religious observance actually entail. This clarification has been forth-
coming at least in regard to the classroom. President Clinton has sought
to address present confusion by circulating guidelines specifying what are
acceptable religious observances in the classroom. Upon announcing the
guidelines, he noted:

> Nothing in the First Amendment converts our public schools
> into religion-free zones or requires all religious expression to
> be left behind at the schoolhouse door. . . . While the gov-
> ernment may not use schools to coerce the consciences of our
> students, or to convey official endorsement of religion, the
> government's schools also may not discriminate against pri-
> vate religious expression during the school day.[15]

These guidelines affirm several practices in the public schools, among
them: individual and informally organized group prayer, the right to
carry and read the Bible and other religious tracts, and the right to wear
religious clothing. They prohibit formally organized school prayer of any
kind, the involvement of teachers and administrators with students in religious activity of any kind, and any attempt by students to proselytize students who have asked them to stop.[16] These guidelines clarify that free
exercise of religious expression is acceptable in the public schools. Similar clarification needs to be made regarding religious observance in other
public contexts as well.

In addition, we need to be better informed about religious diversity
and its significance for the political life and health of this country. There
are at least two ways to become better informed, both of which promote
community rather than divisiveness. One involves the public school system; the other involves the churches.

Whether one is religious or not, the general public would benefit
greatly from formal public education regarding the many different religious traditions observed in this country. This kind of education should
be carefully distinguished from religious education as it is conducted by
religious institutions. We need neither to excise religion from the public
schools nor to indoctrinate. Rather, religion should be taught comparatively, historically, and without prejudice at all levels of public education,
just as other subjects in the humanities and social sciences are presently
taught in the public schools.

This kind of educating already takes place in both public and private
higher education. The people who teach the academic study of religion
in institutions of higher learning are trained experts like those who teach

chemistry, physics, history, and English literature. There is no substantive reason not to extend the same training to those who wish to teach in elementary and secondary education. Just as a good education in world history and U.S. history promotes better citizenship because it fosters a better understanding of where we came from and how we got here, so a better understanding of religious belief and behavior would promote a better understanding of where we are right now. As things presently stand, our public system of education has produced a general population ignorant of the different religious traditions practiced in this country. One further consequence of this general ignorance is a religiously ignorant communications industry that often distorts and misrepresents religious life. Thus, the most serious consequence of all this ignorance is a self-reinforcing process of misunderstanding one of the most vital features of human life.

In addition to formal public education that is comparative, historical, and nonprejudicial, the Christian churches also have a role to play in rectifying this ignorance and misunderstanding. As people of a covenant shared with Jews and Muslims, we need to understand that we participate in injustice when what we do has the consequence of coercing the consciences of others, whether their faiths are religious or secular. We surely would not want others to treat us in such a way. A tradition of covenant reminds us that Christians are called to peace on earth with justice, not to division and tyranny.

In the spirit of seeking a just peace, the churches need to introduce the study of religions other than Christianity into their congregations in the context of dialogue with representatives from various traditions. Indeed some churches have already begun the practice of offering adult Christian education courses in the world's major traditions. In addition, some congregations have sought contact with members of other faiths. For example, every Thanksgiving, the Cathedral of San Fernando in San Antonio, Texas, celebrates with an interreligious service that includes, along with Catholics, Protestants, Jews, Muslims, Buddhists, and Hindus. The service is broadcast internationally through the Catholic Broadcasting Network. For this to become common practice, clergy need to be trained in the seminaries in an understanding of the traditions of other faiths as well as the traditions of their own faith.

The churches also have a central role to play in better educating Christians in Christian traditions themselves. We who are Christian need to pay attention to the theological implications of covenant making, especially the priority of God, in regard to prayer. The priority of God means having no other gods before God. The priority of God has serious direct implications for what it means to worship God in the midst of

Christian diversity, as well as within the particular Christian communities and families to which we belong.

Having no other gods before God requires that Christians better understand Christianity's internal diversity by comprehending that the differences among us are not simply reducible to which Christians are right and which are wrong in regard to teaching and practice. Confidence in one's own traditions will ultimately fail if it rests on being right to the exclusion of all other possibilities, for this is the idolatry of misplaced faith. When we recite the Apostles' Creed, we confess membership in a church that exceeds the boundaries of narrowly defined denominations, as well as participation in a communion of saints reaching back beyond the birth of Jesus himself. When Christians pray together in faith, we pray to God in Jesus the Christ, not to the very human religious organizations and institutions that mediate this reality.

Having no other gods before God moreover entails better understanding the meaning of prayer in our own lives and teaching our children in our churches and our homes, rather than in our schools, what it means to pray. Prayer, to be genuine, must be voluntary rather than forced. Uncoerced prayer is, after all, what religious freedom is all about. Furthermore one who prays, normally prays to God as concretely apprehended through the distinctive symbols of a particular tradition, rather than to a vague abstraction. This is true whether the prayer is spontaneous or part of a daily discipline of faith. Mandating prayer, even for Christians, violates the very meaning of prayer itself.

5

On Behalf of the Children

Rearing children according to the traditions of their parents is itself fraught with problems when the parents' traditions run counter to the prevailing laws and norms of the land. How far does the right of an adult to dissent extend in regard to how he treats his children? Does a parent have responsibilities and obligations to her child that transcend her right to dissent, or does her right to dissent transcend her obligations? These questions become especially difficult when a child's well-being may be at risk because of behavior a parent considers to be in keeping with his religious convictions. Do children have rights, particularly rights to protection from parents who put them at risk on the grounds of the parents' religious convictions? If children do have such rights, under what conditions and how does the state intervene on their behalf? What does a mandate to seek justice require of Christians as covenant makers in response to conflicts between parents and children or between parents and the state over children?

In regard to state intervention in family life, the courts have long debated and disputed the state's right to intervene in family matters in regard to religious practices. This is particularly true where a child's health is threatened. Several cases have appeared before the Supreme Court regarding intervention; examples include Christian Scientist reliance on prayer to heal medical problems and the refusal of Jehovah's Witnesses to allow blood transfusions. In regard to Christian Scientist reliance on prayer, parents have been prosecuted for everything from criminal neglect of a child to manslaughter for the deaths of children who might otherwise have been saved by conventional medicine. While these children might indeed have lived, had their parents not relied solely on prayer and had they sought conventional medical intervention, defense lawyers have pointed out that we do not prosecute parents who turn to medical professionals who nevertheless fail to save the lives of their children. In both cases parents are acting in what they understand to be the best interests of their children. They are not neglecting them, nor do they intend them harm. But what about the children?

The issue of state intervention on behalf of the well-being of children is also central to understanding the decision on the part of Attorney General Janet Reno to authorize the final attack on the Branch Davidian compound in Waco, Texas, in 1993. Concern for sexual and violent abuse of the children, particularly the sexual abuse of female minors, played a major role in Reno's agreement to a raid that ended with the deaths of the very children who were the objects of her concern. Federal officials have yet to acknowledge the full implications of what it means that the Branch Davidians were a voluntary community of families who saw themselves collectively as a family, as opposed to hostages held by a terrorist. The President who appointed these officials, ironically the very President who speaks so eloquently on behalf of America as an all-inclusive family of families, continues to give his full support to the decision to attack the compound. At the same time, evidence of abuse within the compound continues to mount. While child abuse hardly warrants the actual conflagration that occurred, both the abuse and the conflagration demand Christian attention and concern. Once again, what about the children?

The Constitution makes no explicit reference to the rights of parents as parents or to the rights of children. In addition, the laws of the individual states are not only inconsistent with one another, but are also inconsistently applied across cases. When conflicts emerge and the state intervenes, whether the context is religious or not, should Christians concerned for the plight of families respond? Should we seek legislation to acknowledge and protect the rights of children? Of parents? What role, if any, might churches play in reforming government regulation of and intervention in family life? Do the churches have a direct role to play in working through conflicts within the families in their congregations?

The right to bring up one's children according to the traditions of one's faith, without government interference, is a major issue for the Christian Coalition. Parental rights should concern all of us, though not necessarily for the same reasons that they concern the Christian Coalition, for children's rights should engage our attention as well. The problems associated with sustaining the rights and responsibilities of both parents and children illustrate dramatically the failures of both political and religious liberalism and conservatism. Religious liberals have, on the whole, simply not taken up the issues of parental rights and the rights of children. By contrast, well-organized, pro-family religious conservatives have lobbied for parental rights while opposing the extension of legal rights to children.

Meanwhile neither political party has been able to effect or to fund programmatic solutions that fairly resolve conflict between parents and their children. Furthermore, both parties have failed to effect legislation that makes explicit the rights and responsibilities of both parents and the state in protecting the well-being of children. Children are in some cases unnecessarily removed from the homes of their parents and placed in foster care; in other cases they are not removed soon enough to avoid serious tragedy.[1] Thus parents, children, and the state all too often find themselves caught up in a three-way conflict to the detriment of both parents and children.

We know that the rights of parents to raise their children according to the values cherished by the parents can conflict directly with children's rights to well-being and safety. Conflicts arise over what constitutes appropriate discipline for children, what constitutes appropriate sexual behavior in the home, and whether parents or adolescent children have the right to determine control over an adolescent's biological reproduction. Conflict arises in other areas as well. Do parents have the right to withhold medical treatment for their children on the grounds that such treatment violates their religious faith? Do parents have a right to rear a child according to sexual values that are considered deviant by a wider culture? Do parents have a right to restrain adolescent children from practicing traditions of their choice if the traditions are rejected by the parents?

Conversely, do children have a right to conventional medical treatment, irrespective of their parents' wishes, in the event that such treatment would potentially save their lives? Do children have a right to protection from adult behaviors, particularly sexual behaviors espoused on religious grounds, that society deems inappropriate for minor children because they have not yet reached an age of consent? Do children have a right to protection from religiously justified physical battering or confinement as forms of discipline? Do adolescent children possess the same constitutional rights to religious freedom guaranteed to adults? Under what circumstances and by what methods does the state have the right to intervene on behalf of minor children?

These questions are far too complicated to be treated comprehensively in this discussion. They are only further complicated by a long history of episodes in which the state at all levels of government has intervened into family life in disastrous ways. Besides which, there are no easy solutions. Nevertheless, these questions, as well as other related ones, must be raised for any discussion of family values, human freedom, and religious faith to be meaningful.

We are currently addressing such questions very haphazardly in legal courts and in legislatures throughout the country. In addition, voluntary groups, concerned individuals, and international organizations have raised some of these issues with partiality. The Christian Coalition has addressed the issue of parental rights. Hillary Rodham Clinton and others like her have advocated on the behalf of children.[2] The United Nations Committee on the Rights of the Child has presented to the United Nations the *Convention on the Rights of the Child*, a treaty that guarantees fundamental rights to children in the context of their necessary dependence on adults, a treaty yet to be ratified by the United States and vehemently opposed by the Christian Coalition.[3]

As far as I know, however, no one in this country has sat down and tried to work out legislation that comprehends parent-child relations with the goal of establishing the rights and responsibilities of both parents and children. By contrast, other countries have long-established legislation on the books.[4] Moreover, as part of establishing children's rights as persons in their own right rather than the property of their parents, articles 5 and 9 of the *Convention on the Rights of the Child* seek to protect children's relations with their parents from intervention by the state (LeBlanc, 296). Nevertheless, in this country, Christians who advocate for parental rights have for the most part viewed advocates for children as the enemy.[5] Conversely, those who advocate for children, consumed by responding to crisis after crisis, have had little time left to think through legislation that would address the rights and responsibilities of both parents and children.

The result is inconsistent application of vastly differing and sometimes conflicting laws at all levels of government. Two very different examples will illustrate some of the range and the depth of the problems we presently face. The first example has to do with the withholding of medical treatment of children on religious grounds; the second has to do with the government raid on the Branch Davidians at Mt. Carmel in Waco, Texas. The withholding of medical treatment of children on religious grounds is particularly significant because the children involved are infants, toddlers, and younger children—in other words, children who are the most dependent of all children on the judgment of their parents. The raid on Mt. Carmel raises the questions of when, under what conditions, and how government officials should intervene when there is a suspicion of child abuse justified on religious grounds.

Withholding Medical Treatment
on Religious Grounds

Two particular Supreme Court cases establish the right of the government to override the First Amendment guarantee of the free exercise of religion and, where necessary, to intervene in the affairs of the family on behalf of children. *Davis v. Beason* (1890) explicitly subordinated the free exercise of religion to the criminal laws of the country.[6] *Prince v. Massachusetts* (1944) validated the role of the state as *parens patriae* in regard to the protection of children in the areas of health and employment.[7] These two decisions taken together establish the state's authority not only over parents but specifically over their religious practices. Nevertheless, forty-four states currently have religious exemption laws on the books, that is, laws that exempt parents from criminal charges for withholding conventional medical care from their children on religious grounds. So, for example, Jehovah's Witnesses may refuse blood transfusions, and Christian Scientists may seek healing through spiritual means in preference to conventional medical care.

The apparent contradictions between the Supreme Court decisions and the statutes of individual states has produced much confusion. In the state of Massachusetts, Ginger and David Twitchell were prosecuted for the manslaughter of their two-year-old son who died of an obstructed bowel after several days of excruciating pain. The conventional medical practice for such a condition is a simple surgical procedure with a very high success rate. Without such an intervention, sufferers literally strangle on their own excrement. The Twitchells, as Christian Scientists, employed spiritual healing according to the tenets of their faith, rather than conventional medical care for their son. That they loved their son deeply and sought what they understood to be best for him was not subject to dispute. They furthermore understood themselves to be protected by the Massachusetts religious exemption law. Nevertheless, the Twitchells were convicted and sentenced to ten years' probation. The prosecuting attorney saw the conviction as a victory for children's rights; officials of the Church of Christ, Scientist saw it as a violation of the First Amendment.[8]

Not only do state religious exemption laws conflict with criminal laws and with Supreme Court decisions, the Supreme Court itself has not been entirely consistent on this issue. Both *Hermanson v. United States* (1977), a Florida case, and *Minnesota v. McKown* (1992) involve parents who refused medical treatment on religious grounds for their diabetic children. In both cases the children suffered prolonged pain according to the evidence presented during the trials. In *Minnesota v. McKown* medical authorities testified that until two hours prior to the death of the child, the child's life could have been saved. In both cases the parents were prosecuted for violation of criminal laws in states where there were religious exemption laws. In both cases the Supreme Court ruled on behalf of the parents. The Court determined that the state religious exemption laws for both Florida and Minnesota inadequately informed the parents of their vulnerability to criminal prosecution and found that the laws therefore violated the parents' rights to due process. Thus, in spite of earlier rulings that the state had the right to intervene as parent on behalf of a child and that religious practices must be subordinated to criminal laws, the Court ruled on behalf of the parents. In other words, the Court redefined the issue as a matter of due process rather than a conflict of laws and a conflict of rights.

These cases pose deeply troubling questions. In every case parents acted on what they understood to be the child's best interest in the context of their faith. They further acted in keeping with the religious exemption laws of their respective states. Though their conception of healing may seem anachronistic and dangerous to those who assume conventional medical care as normative, medical professionals are themselves increasingly more accepting of alternative practices, like spiritual healing, in conjunction with conventional practices as beneficial in many instances to those who suffer. Furthermore, the scientific community remains ignorant about much that afflicts the human person. The history of medical science includes along with its many successes no small number of failures and mistakes that have cost numerous lives. Yet we do not prosecute parents for the abuse and neglect of their children, when their children die at the hands of medical practitioners. We assume instead that the parents, given what they knew and believed at the time, have acted as best they could on behalf of their children.

But what about the children who in many cases would have in all likelihood survived, if provided with conventional medical care? Is there no way to protect them? If we can require immunization by law, can we not also require the use of conventional medicine that has a proven record of success for underage children? How are we to decide this dilemma? I myself believe that all children have a fundamental right to the best health care available, regardless of cost. At the same time, it is not entirely clear what constitutes the best health care available or who is in the best position to decide on the behalf of children. To my mind we need to be holding summits on this issue throughout the country. These summits would include representation from medical professionals, alternative health-care practitioners, religious professionals, clergy, parents on every side of the issue, most especially parents who have been through the courts on this issue, legal professionals, and children who have been healed by both conventional and alternative means. Within the context of such a summit, present religious exemption laws need to be either rewritten or else removed from the books.

The Branch Davidians, Child Abuse, and the Government Raid on Mt. Carmel

Intervention on the behalf of children played a central role in Attorney General Janet Reno's decision to attack the Branch Davidian compound that tragically ended a fifty-one-day siege. On February 28, 1993, agents from the Bureau of Alcohol, Tobacco, and Firearms raided the Branch Davidian compound known as Mt. Carmel near Waco, Texas, for the purpose of serving a search warrant of the premises and an arrest warrant for David Koresh, the leader of the Branch Davidians. The raid turned into a battle during which four agents and six Branch Davidians were killed. A siege lasting fifty-one days followed. The siege ended April 19, 1993, when the compound went up in flames just hours after FBI tanks shot tear gas into the buildings housing the Branch Davidians. At that time, more than seventy Branch Davidians died either from gunshot wounds or from smoke inhalation. Koresh died from gunshot wounds.

The Branch Davidians initially formed themselves by breaking away from the Seventh-Day Adventists in 1929. The group first called itself the Shepherd's Rod. It continued to hold to the Adventist belief in pacifism and to observe the Adventist practice of a strict vegetarian diet. The founder, Victor Houteff, nevertheless, took issue with the Adventists over when to observe the sabbath. He further differed from the Adventists on when Christ would return, arguing that the return would occur within the year. Though Christ did not return as predicted, the community survived. The group subsequently underwent at least two changes in name, as well as a succession of leaders. The last two of them, Ben Roden and Vernon Wayne Howell, later known as David Koresh, modified the group's theology to justify the use of violence.[9] It was Koresh who introduced the idea of an apocalyptic battle with the U.S. government that would mark the end of the world. According to Koresh's interpretation of the biblical book of Revelation, this battle would occur in Texas.[10] Koresh instituted other changes in addition to the change on violence. He suspended the practice of vegetarianism. He further annulled all marriages within the community, and, claiming that his seed and his alone was divine, he declared himself the only male with rights to sexual intercourse with the women of the compound.[11] Koresh also began to stockpile weapons in anticipation of a final conflict with the federal government that would end in conflagration.

The events leading up to the raid, as well as the events of the raid, the siege, and the final conflagration are subject to dispute. The federal government initially became involved over weapons. The Bureau of Alcohol, Tobacco, and Firearms (ATF) investigated the Branch Davidians for federal weapons violations on the suspicion that they were converting semi-automatic weapons into automatic weapons. The discovery of grenades that were to be shipped to the compound in May 1992 only heightened government suspicions and fears. In response to this discovery, the ATF set up undercover agents in residence in a nearby house for the purpose of surveillance. They infiltrated the compound with an undercover agent as well.[12] To this day the full extent to which federal weapons laws were actually violated remains unclear, though the Branch Davidian male survivors of the events have been tried, and all but one convicted of weapons violations.

In addition to suspicions of violations of federal weapons laws, federal agents also suspected child abuse. Allegations of abuse included the regular and systematic beating of all the children, sexual intercourse by Koresh with minor females, and instructing children in methods to commit suicide, all of which were justified by Koresh on religious grounds. Joyce Sparks, a representative of the Texas Department of Human Services, visited the compound twice and found no evidence of abuse, though she later testified that she thought that she may have been deceived. The social services investigation produced only one concrete allegation charging Koresh with beating a baby, and the investigation was closed on April 30, 1992.[13] For many who opposed the government's involvement at Mt. Carmel, the allegations of abuse were themselves suspect because they were made by members who had left the group. However, according to the later testimony of one of the survivors who appeared before congressional hearings to investigate the events from the initial raid to the conflagration, the women in the compound to whom Koresh had sexual access included girls as young as ten years old.[14] Fear for the safety of the children in the compound played a major role in Attorney General Janet Reno's decision to end the siege on April 19. In only one of many horrible ironies surrounding the events at Waco, the very children she sought to protect died in the conflagration precipitated by the attack of the FBI tanks.

Since the events of 1993, at least two federal investigations have taken place. The first, conducted by the attorney general's office, found that ATF officials had made serious mistakes of judgment that they had later attempted to cover up. The FBI, which also became involved, was exonerated of any wrongdoing. Mistakes of judgment notwithstanding, both Attorney General Reno and President Clinton have continued to insist that the person solely responsible for the fiasco was Koresh. Nevertheless, Mt. Carmel has become a rallying point for heavily armed right-wing militias, as well as a matter of serious concern for civil libertarians and intellectuals committed to due process and to freedom of religion.

Sorting out what violations occurred and who bears responsibility for the fiasco exceeds the scope of this discussion. Nevertheless, to put it as briefly as possible, in my opinion, officials representing the ATF and the FBI, operating out of ignorance and misinformation, fueled by career concerns and sensationalist media coverage, handled the whole affair, including the subsequent investigations, far worse than they have acknowledged. That Attorney General Reno capitulated to pressure because of lack of experience is no excuse. For the leaders of the agencies involved to have responded as if they were paramilitary forces was not only ill informed and unnecessary, but also only further legitimates the fears of those concerned that the United States is a police state.

According to the testimony of the ATF infiltrator, he warned the ATF officials in advance that Koresh knew of the raid and was ready for a standoff. The infiltrator tried to persuade higher-ups that they had lost the element of surprise and should cancel, if they wished to avert tragedy. They disregarded his report and attacked anyway. Later, lawyers for the Branch Davidians testified that Koresh had agreed to surrender within ten to fourteen days, as soon as he finished his interpretation of the meaning of the seventh seal (a reference to the biblical book of Revelation), because God had told him it was okay to come out of the compound once this task was accomplished. The lawyers believed him and cut a deal with the FBI to give Koresh the time needed to complete his task. Instead, the FBI reneged and launched the attack using tanks and tear gas that ended in the conflagration. The FBI argued that, having detected evidence of tuberculosis in the compound and realizing that health conditions were rapidly deteriorating (there were no indoor toilets), agents felt they had to step up activity and decided to end the siege accordingly to save the lives of the children.[15]

Both the infiltrator and the lawyers were party to more than one perspective in forming their judgments of the situation. Both the infiltrator and the lawyers had direct contact with Koresh in contexts in which Koresh did not perceive them as the enemy; thus, he could respond in ways that differed from his responses to the agents who besieged him. This difference allowed the infiltrator and the lawyers a sense of what they found to be his credibility, an attribute automatically denied him by the federal agents. When asked why they believed Koresh, given his religious beliefs, one lawyer replied, in marked contrast to the agents, that he did not judge a man's credibility by the religious doctrines he held. Though both the infiltrator and the lawyers were members of normative culture and shared common assumptions like "the world is probably not going to end tomorrow," they had direct access to the people whose beliefs were not only radically different, but highly questionable in relation to society's norms. This access appears to have allowed them to imagine a world alien to them without demonizing it. This "double" position of being within society, yet able to imagine a different social context, put them in the privileged position of granting humanity and rights to a group to whom most people were responding by demonizing them as terrorists and crazies. It is precisely the demonization of Koresh for his religious beliefs that set up the possibility for the final attack on the compound. Koresh was likely guilty of criminal offenses ranging from child abuse to weapons violations, for which he should have been arrested and prosecuted accordingly. Instead, because of the reactions of normal people to his religious beliefs, both government agents and Branch Davidians died violently and unnecessarily.

In short, operating out of questionable assumptions about the people with whom they were dealing, government agents violated at the very least the group's constitutional rights of free assembly, free exercise, and due process in a manner that contributed to the deaths of almost ninety people in the process. However, just as the possible outrages and crimes committed by Branch Davidians in no way deserved the response they got, likewise, the ineptitude and excesses of government agencies do not warrant the extremism of the right-wing militias who fancy themselves as true revolutionaries while keeping the National Rifle Association in business. Nor should the events at Mt. Carmel serve to justify past and future abuses perpetrated by the anticult movement in the name of religious orthodoxy. Waco is a national tragedy for which Koresh, his followers, the popular media, the anticult movement, the ATF, the FBI, and the attorney general's office all bear responsibility.[16]

The charges of child abuse make this tragedy an issue of family values. The Branch Davidians constituted a religious community that saw itself as a voluntary family of which Koresh was the head. The community included conventionally defined families, that is, adults who had mar-

ried and reproduced offspring. These adults consented to and participated in the questionable treatment of their children. The charges of
child abuse rest on the testimony of people who had left the group, as well
as the testimony of a survivor, released from the compound with other
children prior to the FBI attack that ended in the fire. This testimony as-
serts that parents consented to Koresh's sexual practices with their
daughters and participated in severe forms of punishment of their children, as well as instructing the children in how to commit suicide in response to the predicted Armageddon.

While there are all kinds of problems with the credibility of many of
the witnesses, I find very credible the testimony of the fourteen-year-old
female who appeared before congressional hearings in the summer of 1995.
In a language noteworthy for its understatement, she described in extended
detail her first sexual interaction with Koresh at the age of ten. Rather than
calling the event a rape or violation, she talked about how she expected it
as part of the normal course of her life. She further described how she did
not particularly enjoy the sexual encounter, as well as subsequent encounters, in a bone-chilling and matter-of-fact tone. My point is that, as a ten-
year-old child, she assumed such behavior was normal behavior in her religious family. And why shouldn't she? After all, her mother consented to
Koresh's treatment of the child.[17] Furthermore, her mother consented out
of religious conviction.

Though some may argue that such examples represent an aberration
and are exceptional, cases of adults abusing their children on religious
grounds are not unusual. One need only read the daily papers and follow
the nightly news. A fundamentalist preacher, citing scriptural passages as
justification, sexually brutalizes both his male and female children as well
as his wife. Another father beheads his son because he believes him to be
possessed by the devil. A stepfather active in the Christian Coalition sexually molests his stepdaughter from her adolescence into her early adulthood.[18] While admittedly the media go out of their way to sensationalize
such cases, they do not fabricate them out of nothing. Furthermore, if
asked, perhaps each of these parents might have claimed to be acting in
the best interests of the children involved.

Such cases differ from those involving the withholding of medical
treatment from children on religious grounds in this respect. Whereas
various individual states have religious exemption laws on the books in
regard to medical treatment, no such exemption laws exist in regard to
physical and sexual behavior. However, as in the case of healing, what precisely constitutes child abuse needs conceptual clarification, particularly
when placed in a religious context. For example, what precisely constitutes

physical battering? Is all corporal punishment abuse? Or, if one spares the rod, does one spoil the child? While most adults would agree that beating a child senseless is unacceptable, adults disagree strongly over spanking and other forms of corporal punishment. Likewise, what constitutes inappropriate sexual behavior within the family? Nudity? A family bed? Fondling? Genital penetration?

Advocacy on Behalf of Children

These questions are tough enough to address on strictly secular grounds; introducing the element of religious conviction only further complicates them. Nevertheless, the Christian Coalition currently seeks legislation protecting, without restriction, parents' rights to bring up their children according to their own religious values and beliefs. Steve Largent (Republican representative from Oklahoma) and Mike Parker (Democratic representative from Missouri), along with Senators Charles Grassley (Republican from Iowa) and Howard Heflin (Democrat from Alabama), are presently crafting a Parental Rights Act. The purpose of the act is to ensure parents' rights to control over children's education, health care, discipline, and religious training. The act further stipulates that government intervention be justified by "clear and convincing evidence," that the intervention be "essential to accomplish a compelling governmental interest," and that the government intervene by "the least restrictive means."[19] As presently described in the *Contract with the American Family*, there are no constraints placed on these practices, no attention to the obligations of parents to their children, nor any reference to the rights of children. The underlying assumption appears to be that children, like other kinds of property, simply belong to their parents.

Furthermore, the criteria for government intervention are ridden with flaws. For example, what would have constituted clear and convincing evidence of child abuse at Mt. Carmel? In fact, a social worker visited twice and found no such evidence. In the case of the man who beheaded his son, the clear and convincing evidence came too late to prevent the death of the son, though it may have saved the lives of his siblings. Moreover, what constitutes a compelling governmental interest in regard to how parents treat their children? Under the Religious Freedom Restoration Act of 1994, the government already has to show compelling interest in order to override the right to free exercise of adults in regard to their own behavior. In regard to how parents treat their children, in *De Shaney v. Winnebago* (1989), in a secular context, the Supreme Court disgracefully ruled so narrowly on compelling interest that it ruled against

state intervention in favor of a father who beat his child senseless.[20] What
then does stipulating this criterion add that does not already exist as law
in regard to parent-child relations? And if the government determines
that it has a clear and compelling interest, what does it mean to intervene
by the least restrictive means possible? Restrictive on whom, the parents,
the children, or both? Most important, why should the religious practices
of parents allow them to treat their children differently in regard to the
law of the land from nonreligious parents or parents whose religious
views do not run counter to the law? Will applying the rod to avoid spoil-
ing the child fall under the free exercise of religion or under discipline?
Are all children, regardless of being minors, entitled as persons to certain
fundamental rights irrespective of their parents' religious convictions?
Are parents bound to meet certain fundamental obligations to their children? Should these obligations be codified as law? The frequency of abuse,
justified on religious grounds, provides a powerful argument against the
legislation currently suggested by the Christian Coalition, unless and until it is accompanied by legislation clearly protecting children from abu-
sive parents.

Rather than crafting what would be tantamount to more religious exemption laws that could foster child abuse, Christians need to be at the
forefront of advocating for the protection of all children, regardless of
what kind of household, religious or otherwise, they come from. We
ought to circulate among the congregations the *Convention on the Rights
of the Child* for study and discussion so that laypeople may decide for
themselves the merits of the document. As Christians we should work together to find ways to help parents in distress who seek alternatives to
abusing their children in the name of disciplining them. As parents we
need to educate ourselves and our children regarding the rights and responsibilities to each other. We should actively support legislation to this
effect. In short, Christians need to negotiate covenants that link rights
with responsibilities for both parents and children.

There are alternative models for the treatment of children within the
family and the government's role in family life. For example, in 1981, the
government of Norway established the position of Ombudsman for Children to advocate officially for children's rights. By 1989 the person fill-
ing this position had played a central role in accomplishing a number of
changes in legislation on behalf of children, including legislation prohibiting corporal punishment, as well as any other treatment of children
threatening their physical or psychological development (Flekkoy, 181).
Furthermore, Norwegian national policy provides a safety net for families that guarantees housing, education, medical care, and other forms of

welfare during periods of economic distress. This safety net works to prevent violence in the home due to stress outside the home and provides important at-home services for sensitizing parents to children's legal rights as persons (Flekkoy, 40–47). Given the significant differences between the two countries, it is unlikely that such a model could be transplanted without modification from Norway to the United States. Nevertheless, what the Norwegians have accomplished provides us a model to build on at the levels of state and local government more suitable to the particularities of our various communities.

The Norwegians can furthermore serve as a model for the churches on a voluntary level. For example, churches could institute or reinstitute the practice of naming godparents at the birth of a child. At the initiative of prospective parents, godparents could sit down with the parents and work out a covenant arrangement whereby they all undergo training that enhances their parental skills. Godparents would further agree to sustained, committed involvement early on that supported parents as they adjusted to the new life in the home. Throughout the upbringing of their child, parents would agree to call their godparents during moments of crisis, particularly if at risk of losing self-control in the midst of a parent-child conflict. The godparents would likewise agree to intervene at such points as nonjudgmental arbitrators on behalf of the best interests of both the children and the parents involved. Given the kind of time commitment involved on the part of the godparents, they would in all likelihood be older adults. Given the goals of nurture and nonviolence, career-oriented parents of both genders would need to think carefully how their goals as parents would interact with their career goals and adjust accordingly. With careful planning and full support by the congregations, churches could effect a revolution in child-rearing practices on a purely voluntary basis.

Conclusion

National legislation jointly establishing and protecting the rights of both parents and children, state legislation to provide at-home help with the rearing of children, and the redefinition of the roles and practices of godparents are only first steps in addressing conflict between parents, between parents and children, and between parents and the state. By themselves these activities will not eliminate all violence in the home, nor all state misintervention into family life. However, they provide first steps that seek to do justice for the "least of these" (Matthew 25:40), whether parents or children. By extending covenantal responsibilities and rights to include children, these first steps acknowledge that children, even if not yet adults, are nevertheless persons rather than the property of their parents, and as persons, worthy of rights and capable of taking responsibilities commensurate with their development.

The problems we face in trying to understand the place of religious life for families are vast in number and complicated in nature. Addressing these problems requires enormous commitments of energy and time. We face rethinking from the ground up the very concept of rights when it comes to parent-child relations, as well as introducing the concept of obligations between parents and children. The Ten Commandments call us to honor our parents that our days may be long on the land (Exodus 20:12), and indeed we should. Should we not honor our children as well?

All the same, every generation has faced difficult tasks involving redefining family life. What distinguishes this generation from its predecessors lies in the sheer diversity of religious and secular traditions that our population observes and in the public nature of the problems we confront. In the past it was relatively safe to assume that most people were religious and that their religious faith was predominantly Christian, most likely Protestant. In the past, religious scandals involving family life were less likely to undergo public scrutiny. Religious homogeneity and domestic privacy, however, no longer characterize national life.

As for the problem of time, somehow, after plowing the north forty or working all day in the factory or washing the clothes by hand, mending them, and ironing them while preparing meals and scrubbing floors, our forebears managed to devote time to reforming the institutions on which they depended in ways that would nourish future existence. Like them, we will not somehow magically find the time, after all our other work is done, to effect needed change in the institutions that are supposed to nourish family life. Rather, as a covenant-making people, we must *make* the time to reform these institutions, from our institutions of education, government, industry, jurisprudence, and communication to the church itself. Such work is every bit as important as the work that we do for economic survival and the energy we exert to keep family relationships flourishing. If we pay attention to the covenants that have shaped our faith, we will find that they provide both substantive guidelines and strategies for confronting the tasks we face.

The substantive guidelines are simple. The prohibition against idolatry prohibits us from elevating our finite forms of worship and our finite family values to the status of absolute. We must take great care to prevent the establishment of a state religion by legislating our own particular observances or by modifying the ceremonial practices of civil religion into distinctively Christian practices in the context of public education, either by intention or by effect. The guideline to seek justice, especially for the outcast, prohibits us from supporting practices and legislation that violate both the rights of those vulnerable to abuse and the rights of those whose religious practices we find at best strange and at worst despicable. This guideline holds regardless of whether the legislation and practices are initiated by the state or by a particular religious group. Where the rights of children and adults conflict, every effort must be made first and foremost to protect those who cannot protect themselves, namely, the children. As we saw in the case of Waco, however, the two sets of rights are often intertwined. Had the government protected the constitutional rights of the adult Branch Davidians more carefully, the children might be alive today.

The primary strategy is democracy itself. Though God may have used Moses and Jesus as emissaries, God made the covenants with all the people present, as well as with future generations. Though covenants made with God are not among equals, the men who stood before God stood among equals, and this equality has extended over time to become more and more inclusive. Covenants made solely among people are covenants made by equals. The political and religious covenants that we presently make to effect change in the human arena must likewise be made of the people, by the people, and for the people. As we struggle concretely with the problems we face, it is easy to forget that we are our government, that therefore everyone who lives with the consequences of reform must have the opportunity to become involved in the process of determining precisely what change will take place. This means that both faith and politics become simultaneously more local and more global, and it is to this issue that we finally turn.

6

Building
Community Today

The differences among Christians are often as wide and deep as the differences that distinguish Christian faith from other faiths. The differences between Wallis and Reed, both of whom are evangelical Protestants, serve as a prime example. All these differences among faiths and within Christian faith pose difficult questions for Christians themselves, questions that inform the conflict surrounding family life. To what kinds of lives does God call us as Christians who are also members of families and citizens of a secular, religiously plural, democratic republic? How do we remain true to that which gives Christian identity its distinctiveness, while preserving a space for difference that allows real relations among people of diverse religious and secular faiths? Given the strife that family issues generate among Christians and between Christians and non-Christians, how might we nevertheless seek to build community in our political and spiritual lives rather than destroy it?

No one can presume to speak for all Christians. Even as a theologian I can only speak from the perspective of the tradition I seek to represent, a tradition that is currently subject to contention among its own adherents. I speak from a Reformed Protestant tradition that holds that even faith itself is a gift and that every word I utter is conditioned by my finitude. This does not mean, however, that I cannot speak out, from the perspective of my own finite faith. On the contrary, my faith requires it.

My tradition further requires of me that I seek answers to these difficult questions by turning to scripture, a scripture read invariably in light of an intervening history and the times in which the reader finds herself. To ask what God requires of us in response to family issues means for me to ask how, according to scripture, Jesus lived as a member of a family and how he responded to those concerns that troubled the people around him in regard to their families. It means to ask further how churches become families and what kind of families they become. It means to push even harder and ask what meaning Jesus' life and the history of the churches has for us as Christians and family members today.

Having raised throughout this book what I consider to be some of the most critical and pressing issues surrounding public discussion of family life, I now conclude by offering a positive theological alternative to the excesses of the extreme, politically activist, Christian right and to the neglect and mistakes of liberal Christianity and liberal politics. This last chapter articulates a theological framework that provides an alternative to the identification of religion and state through family values that occurs on both sides of the political fence. It explores Jesus' ambivalence toward families, the churches' historic assumption and extension of the role of family, the present place of the churches as shapers and receptacles of faith as members of a wider earth household, and the promising role the churches might play today in building coalitions within and across religious and secular communities.

Going through Jesus to Get to God

Christian faith is faith in God mediated by Jesus the Christ. Faith in God distinguishes Christian faith from nontheistic, polytheistic, and secular forms of faith. That Jesus mediates this faith distinguishes it from other monotheistic faiths. The figure of Jesus mediates faith in many different ways among Christian communities. Some Christians focus predominantly on personal relationship to Jesus as redemptive. Others seek to live in faith according to Jesus' teachings and his vision of God's coming rule on earth; for them redemption lies in social transformation of this earth. Still others focus primarily on tradition itself. In any case, the figure of Jesus in some way reveals who God is, such that those who call themselves Christian come to trust that God is and that God's love creates all that is and redeems all it touches. In other words, "Christian" means going through Jesus to get to God.

What patterns may we discern that reveal Jesus' values with regard to family relations and life? I find ambivalence on Jesus' part. On the one hand, Jesus challenges the limits of family ties defined by bloodlines; on the other hand, he uses metaphors drawn from family life to talk about the fellowship that emerges around him.

For example, the Gospels consistently portray Jesus' rejection of biological ties as definitive of family. Throughout the Gospels Jesus calls on God, not Joseph, as *Abba*, commonly translated into English as "father," but more accurately rendered as "daddy." At points in the Gospel narratives, he rejects his own biological family's claims on him (Mark 3:34–35). He calls on others to leave their families and to follow him (Luke 9:60). In addition to rejecting the claims of his biological family, he challenges Levitical regulations governing marriage and divorce (Matthew 5:31–32), and proclaims a coming age, marked by family members turning against one another (Mark 13:12–13). Most significant, Jesus rejects calling any man "father" (Matthew 23:9). The apostle Paul continues this challenge to a conventional understanding of family ties in a similar vein by recommending marriage only as the lesser of two evils (1 Corinthians 7:8–9). Thus many of the earliest Jewish followers and the later emerging Gentile communities saw themselves as families that stood as alternatives to male-dominated, biologically generated families.[1]

At the same time, according to the Gospel narratives, Jesus' own family life as well as his treatment of other people affirms unconventional families and family ties under certain conditions. These ties become the framework for establishing as families the new communities that emerge on his death. According to tradition Jesus is born under circumstances that call into question his legitimacy. His mother appears to be at risk of becoming an unwed mother; nevertheless, her fiancé Joseph stands by her and assumes responsibilities for a paternity for which he has no biological authority (Matthew 1:18–25). During Jesus' earliest childhood, his small family flees the pursuit of government officials who seek to kill him on behalf of Herod (Matthew 2:1–15). In his adulthood, Jesus himself exhibits special concern for unconventional families—for widows, children, and members cast out of conventional families because of illness or divorce (respectively, Mark 12:42; Mark 10:14; Mark 1:40–45; and John 4:7–26). He furthermore clearly envisions himself in the role of mother, weeping over Jerusalem (Luke 13:34). Moreover, he proclaims a kingdom likened to a family in which the prodigal son is joyously welcomed back into the family to share in its wealth (Luke 15:11–32). Last but not least, he calls upon his followers to identify as sisters and brothers with those who suffer, and he promises that God is to be found among the suffering and the afflicted (Matthew 25:31–46). This bond finds one of its deepest symbolic expressions in the fellowship of breaking bread and drinking wine together (Mark 14:12–25). For Paul this community becomes the very body of Christ (1 Corinthians 12:12–31). Participation in this body further binds Christians to Christ as their brother and supersedes all biological and social ties to family (Romans 8:12–17).

The relationship between the familial community Jesus established and the Roman state was disruptive to both. A Palestinian Jewish teacher who went on the road, Jesus, even as he sought to live Torah, challenged both religious and civil authorities.[2] The Roman state prosecuted, convicted, and executed him, apparently for treason. Some of his own followers betrayed and denied him. Under ordinary circumstances he, like Toni Morrison's Beloved, would have been forgotten. Nevertheless, some of his ragtag little band of followers, notably his female followers, refused to let his vision die, proclaiming that he and therefore the vision triumphed over death itself (Mark 15:1–16:8).

Among other things, Jesus claimed that we are all children of a God who loves us, whose love makes just love possible among us. This love is as intimately and directly connected to human existence as a child's existence is ideally speaking intimately and directly connected to that of his or her parents. This love also heals by disruption—disruption of all conventional configurations of power that define the state, religious institutions, and the family; it further sustains the people and institutions who encounter it by turning their normal expectations upside down, inside out, and backward in ways that produce both fear and joy (Luke 1:46–55). This love exceeds the bounds of its own particularism even in the midst of what appears to be Jesus' own exclusivism.

In the Gospel according to John, Jesus claims to be the only way to relationship with God as *Abba* (John 14:6). This claim lends Christian faith its distinctive identity as Christian in two respects. First, the claim establishes Jesus' role as a mediator of faith in God. In order to have the faith that establishes a particular kind of intimacy with God, one must acknowledge Jesus as brother and friend. Those outside of Jewish traditions would have had no access to the God of Abraham, Sarah, Isaac, Rebekah, Jacob, Leah, Rachel, and the whole cloud of Jewish witnesses (Hebrews 11:1–12), and certainly no access to this kind of intimacy with God, without this mediation. Second, what Jesus mediates is a highly intimate relationship best understood symbolically in terms of the relations between a parent and a child. *Abba* is a term of endearment that is better translated "daddy," because it is far less formal than "father" conveys in English. Thus, the distinctiveness of Jesus' claim regarding God is that the God who creates and redeems is accessible to human beings in the way that nurturing parents are accessible to their children.

Distinctiveness notwithstanding, is the claim an exclusivist one? Only if taken out of its wider context. Furthermore, what Jesus does not say is as important as what Jesus does say. The wider context of the Gospel includes Jesus' reference to "many dwelling places" in God's house to which Jesus goes to prepare "a place" for his followers (John 14:2–3). "Many dwelling places," taken in conjunction with "a place" designated among them for the followers, implies that there is room for others in addition to the followers who come to know God through Jesus as daddy. In addition, Jesus does not claim that there is only one kind of relationship with God or that there is only one kind of intimacy with God. Rather, Jesus claims that he is the only way to a particular kind of intimacy with God. We know from other Gospels and from the epistles that Jesus and the members of the early community drew on their legacy of images from Hebrew Bible and their immediate surroundings as resources to symbolize human-divine relations. The novelty of what Jesus does is to talk about human-divine relations in an unconventional way, namely, as a highly intimate parent-child relationship. Addressing God as daddy adds to an already existing, rich legacy of metaphors, including God as breath, spirit, lord, king, warrior, woman in labor, wisdom, and friend, just as later images for God would emerge like lover, dove, fire, and word. The extraordinary thing that subsequently happens is that his followers make monotheistic faith available to Gentiles.

At the same time, the "way" of which Jesus speaks is in more general terms God's very own love, a love that cannot be bound by the finitude of time and space, including Jesus' own time and space. Thus unconditional love pushes beyond its own necessary historicity, past, present, and future, pushing the believer caught up in it beyond the exclusivist confines of institutional and familial loyalties. Jesus' claim to be the only way to God at once distinguishes Christian *faith* from other faiths and supersedes specifically *Christian* faith. This massive contradiction that God's love is unconditional, even as it is historically conditioned, produces an inevitable and irresolvable tension within Christian faith between the particularity of its origins and the universality of its intentions. One could write the subsequent history of Christian life and institutions in terms of how this tension plays itself out in Christians' relations with other Christians and with those of other religious and secular faiths.

From my perspective, the God Jesus gets us to connects us all to one another in celebration of our particularity and difference in ways that extend us beyond ourselves to welcome others. This revelation that we are interconnected as the people of God in the midst of our diversity supersedes any attempts to exclude others, whether in the name of Jesus, in the name of the church, or in the name of faith itself. Jesus' ambivalence toward family, defined along biological and social lines in terms of marriage, reproduction, and the rearing of children, is well founded. For family structures often reinforce loyalties that preclude kindness to outcasts and strangers and further inhibit respect for enemies and for neighbors with whom we disagree. Those who find their faith in God through Jesus would do well to sustain the same ambivalence.

The subsequent Christian churches have preserved Jesus' ambivalence toward the family with more and less success. For example, in addition to validating heterosexual marriages and reproduction, as well as monastic orders and house churches, early Christian communities included orders of widows, thus providing economic and spiritual care for an otherwise abandoned class of women. Moreover, the church of the Middle Ages later validated the choice to remain single by establishing religious orders of celibates, symbolically structured as brides of Christ, for both men and women.

These orders were of special importance to women, for they provided women alternatives to arranged marriages, as well as access to education and to some small degree of power to decide the shapes of their own lives. These early communities furthermore not only defined themselves as brotherhoods and sisterhoods, many of them sought to model themselves spiritually, economically, and socially on their perception of the kingdom of God proclaimed in the gospels. Thus, the churches affirmed not only family life established along blood-determined kinship lines but also established social, voluntary kinship among those who rejected marriage and reproduction. These different manifestations of actual and metaphorical families stood in hierarchical relation to one another in ways that were consistently oppressive to women and to some men; for example, church authorities with few exceptions denied believers rights to control over reproduction, to divorce, and to sexual practices outside the context of reproduction. Nevertheless, believers had some choice from a number of available lifestyles.[3]

With the Protestant Reformation most Protestant women lost sanction for the choice to remain single, though many Protestant denominations are now more accepting of divorce and of sexual pleasure apart from reproduction, provided it derives from heterosexual practices. With few exceptions even today, however, most Protestant women continue to derive their status from heterosexual marriage. In the past, exceptions occurred within some historical communities, often separatist or millenarian, like the Anglicans, who established religious orders for women, and the Shakers, all of whose members practiced celibacy.

Regardless of what form Christian churches have historically taken or of what choices they have availed their congregants, the churches have drawn on the Gospels, as well as on the epistles, as resources for understanding themselves as institutions as mother of the people of God, who together form a family. In addition, preachers, theologians, and mystics have exhorted believers to assume the role of mother as individuals in relation to Christ. So, for example, Jonathan Edwards urged believers to nurture the infant Christ within them, even as the church nurtures them.[4] Regardless of who is mothering whom, the church as a community of mutual nurturers, called to extend nurture beyond its own boundaries, is a recurring theme throughout Christian history. This theme carries over into the present as witnessed by Miller-McLemore's proposal that all believers seek to become mothers or the people who care (185–95). While the church as family has often manifested itself in male-dominated, exclusive, militant terms, there are coexisting, more fruitful manifestations, both actual and possible.

Christian Faith in a Land of Many Faiths

The church as a family in its own right constitutes only one family among many, however. The existence of multiple faiths represented, both actually and metaphorically, by multiple families raises the tough question of the place of Christian faith in relation to other faiths. In the past the relation of Christian faith to other faiths has evoked defensiveness and assertions of superiority among Christians, in part grounded in Jesus' own claim to be the only way to God, interpreted out of context. Defensiveness and concern with superiority, often linked with national and political agendas, have produced a bloody history that cannot easily be separated from faith itself, for faith cannot be isolated in pure form from the violence of its context. Furthermore, those same connections between faith and national will characterize the political and religious discourse of this country today. This particular linkage of faith and politics requires a response that is both theological and political, a response that can affirm Christian faith in its own distinctiveness, even as it challenges Christian attempts to establish domination over others.

The issue of superiority relates to the issue of domination. I shall focus first on the issue of superiority. Is Christian faith superior to other faiths? This question, read in its best light, stems from misplaced loyalty in the midst of a world of many faiths and doubts. The very word "superiority" assumes a competition, more appropriate to sports and to business than to Christian faith. Concern with superiority reflects our sinfulness in that it arises from a suspicion of others who are different, a need to be "special," and an inability to accept God's grace.

The question of whether Christian faith is superior to other faiths arises partly from a suspicion of those who differ from us. This suspicion

leads quickly to an assertion of domination. In the past, Christian responses both to internal differences and to external ones have produced
serious, often violent conflict. Some of this conflict represents attempts
to prove that Christian faith, or even a particular kind of Christian faith,
is superior. From the Inquisition to the execution of Servetus, from the
Crusades to missionary practices that destroyed the cultures of tribal peo-
ples, from Christians who supported slavery to Christians who blow up
abortion clinics, these attempts have come back to haunt later Christians
as shameful moments of violation of the very gospel we have sought to
proclaim and to practice. The question of religious superiority can serve
and historically has served as a first step toward refusing to revere the image of God in all others, irrespective of their religious or nonreligious
practices and convictions.

The question of religious superiority may conversely arise from a
need to feel unique, to see oneself as different from others. Unfortunately, we often confuse uniqueness with being special at the expense of
others. After all, the values of our culture place heavy emphasis on distinguishing ourselves by winning, coupled with upward mobility all the
way to the top of the social ladder. Given some Calvinist views of election, Reformed Protestants are particularly tempted by such values. The
most serious difficulty lies in a lack of awareness that uniqueness is a gift
available to all, not the possession of some to the exclusion of others.
These cultural temptations, theologically rationalized, make it increasingly harder to feel confident in one's uniqueness without denying simultaneously the uniqueness or distinctiveness of other individuals and
communities.

Lastly, Christians, no less than others, have serious difficulty accepting gifts, especially gifts from God, and in response to them, living a life
of joy and gratitude without needing to measure or to compare. The good
news is that God's gracious rule has broken through our sinfulness in
spite of our resistance, to fill us with an exuberantly joyous love that we
can neither contain nor control, but can only pass on. We have only to
repent and to trust this grace to become participants in a new reality oriented toward justice with mercy. From a Reformed Protestant perspective this trust or faith is itself a gift of God, granted to us as Gentiles
through the life, death, and resurrection of Jesus the Christ. In other
words, Jesus' faith makes our faith possible. It is this new reality to which
we are called that should attract us, not the hell we escape, who is in and
who is out, or the order in which we entered.

We unfortunately turn even this gift into an act of idolatry when we
proclaim that Jesus alone is the true revelation of God, a claim best articu-

lated in this century by theologian Karl Barth and further proclaimed in the Barmen Declaration.[5] According to Barth, God has uniquely and solely revealed Godself through Jesus the Christ; there is no other definitive revelation of God. Barth argues that all religion, including Christianity, is idolatry. Nevertheless, God's gracious self-revelation through Jesus the Christ marks Christian faith as the one true faith in spite of Christian tendencies to idolatry. The Barmen Declaration reflects the same position. In agreement with Barth, Barmen rejects any possibility for divine revelation outside of Jesus the Christ, a point with which I take issue.

I agree that Jesus is *a* unique revelation of God and that Jesus as God's self-revelation is definitive for Christian faith. I likewise think that all religion is subject to idolatry. The Barmen Declaration takes a very strong stand on the separation of church and state, which I endorse wholeheartedly. It furthermore affirms Trinitarian orthodoxy as central to Christian identity, with which I concur. Nevertheless to me the claim that Christian faith is uniquely true, Christianity's idolatry notwithstanding, on the grounds that Jesus is the *sole*, *definitive* revelation of God constitutes the ultimate act of idolatry, for it limits God's power to determine God's self-revelation. To make such a claim is to presume to have God's knowledge. This claim furthermore presumes that people of faith who are not Christians are living an illusion or a lie, for they are excluded from access to truth.

I do not appreciate when representatives from other religious traditions (as well as other Christian denominations) make similar claims regarding my tradition; my faith itself prohibits me from turning around and doing the same thing to someone from a tradition different from my own. The theologian H. Richard Niebuhr represents an alternative point of view when he argues that Jesus provides Christians with a particular image of an all-inclusive God, but not the only image.[6] This view allows for more than one way to a truth that redeems. I am persuaded by Niebuhr's view rather than Barth's. I would only add that there exists more than one truth as well. In any case, if God's grace is real in our lives, the question of superiority, based on access to an exclusive truth, is meaningless. Once the question becomes meaningless, the need to dominate may dissolve, unless, of course, it is embedded in a political agenda.

Once the question of superiority becomes meaningless, we are freed as Christians to engage with a world that is both secular and religiously plural without apology for our faith. We are free to encounter people of many different faiths as human beings from whom we have much to learn, to whom we hopefully have much to give, and with whom we have much to share. Rather than seeking to transform others by challenging their faith as illusory, we should simply, humbly bear witness to our faith in how we live our lives. Indeed, our own faith may be strengthened by engaging in dialogue as we come to understand just where our real differences lie and what their full significance really is. I do not mean that there will be no conflict, nor do I intend to proclaim a sentimental view of interreligious dialogue. On the contrary, my experience of such dialogues is that they are difficult, very challenging struggles in seeking to understand others on their own terms—struggles that strike me as preeminently faithful responses to those whom we perceive to differ from us. But interreligious dialogue can also be invigorating and in any case is necessary to building bridges in a pluralistic society that is deeply fractured by anger and violence, in short, this society. In the long run, I think we have much more to fear from an exclusivist view of Christian faith than we have to fear from encountering and delighting in many of our religious differences.[7]

By virtue of the *imago Dei*, the people of God include all people regardless of their religious or irreligious convictions. Christian commitment to decent and just family life must extend far beyond the particular immediate families and the particular religious loyalties of Christians. Most Christian women and men fulfill multiple roles as family members, workers, friends, and citizens. These roles take us outside the confines of our particular communities of faith. Nevertheless, if we are true to our faith, we carry it with us. We live in a secular, religiously and culturally diverse democratic republic, governed by laws that attempt to preserve this diversity. As citizens who are Christian we are, along with others, responsible for this democratic republic, a responsibility that includes preserving this diversity "with liberty and justice for all." Moreover, our citizenship extends even farther than national boundaries to embrace the whole earth as God's creation; as Christians we have responsibilities to other forms of life and to future human generations as well.

The Fallacy of Mainstream and Margin

Secularity, religious pluralism, and care for the earth have serious implications for Christian faith as practiced in a political arena. Secularity and religious pluralism in the context of democracy demand of us that we practice the values of our faith in ways that leave a special kind of room for difference—a room for difference that allows genuine relations among the people of this country in all our diversity.[8] Creating this space means giving up divisions like *mainstream* and *margin*, rather than fighting over whose values will dominate as mainstream. This is no small task. It requires a total overhaul of attitude from intellect to emotions, a revolution of the heart or what Jesus called *metanoia* (Mark 1:15).[9] It means listening with compassion as well as speaking out—listening to others without trying to change them or their lifestyles to fit our expectations. It means openness to possibilities that we can neither know in advance nor control altogether, once we discover or invent them. These virtues of listening well, openness to an unknown future, and giving up immediate control do not normally characterize Protestant activism in either its liberal or its conservative manifestations. Nor do these virtues characterize the stereotypic "can do" robustness of the national character that many nostalgically think of as mainstream. Indeed, who is in control and whether such a mainstream exists or even should exist are in large part what the contention over family life is all about.

Meanwhile, the end of the Cold War is producing a revolution in political structures around the world. The revolution in this country manifests itself presently in the breakdown and fragmentation of both liberal and conservative politics in a multitude of ways. Many disaffected citizens are abandoning both political parties either to remain politically active as independents or simply to drop out of civic life altogether. Those who maintain their traditional party affiliations scramble to redefine these political traditions in ways that are sometimes more fitting to present times, but most often in ways that simply pander to the loudest and apparently most powerful voices speaking at the time. From the family to the church to the government the issue is control. What Patrick Buchanan describes as cultural warfare extends far beyond issues of culture to pervade every area of human life. In the midst of this fragmentation and struggle for control, Christians would do well to keep in mind the twin dangers of remaining silent in the face of injustice and of introducing further division on sectarian grounds.

For example, family values, whatever their content, if they are theologically or religiously grounded, should not be identified with a national will, either by the political and religious right or by the political and religious left. Such an identification not only goes against the grain of religious and political pluralism preserved by the Bill of Rights, but, from a theological perspective, it elevates finite values to infinite status and thus constitutes idolatry. Nevertheless both the left and the right make this identification, albeit in different ways, and few people appear to be speaking out against it.

A moderated version of the Christian Coalition's usually even more extreme view of family values, the *Contract with the American Family* serves as an example of the excesses of the religious and political right. This contract elevates the values of a particular class, race, gender, and culture as if they were both definitively Christian and mainstream, while excluding those families that do not fit its narrow definition of *family*. Both the elevation and the exclusion are antithetical to Christian teaching and to a democratic system that seeks to protect dissent.

In regard to the excesses of the political left, the use of a rhetoric of family values has reinforced a tendency on the part of government to overreact and to intervene inappropriately in family and religious life, as witnessed by the government siege at Waco. Whereas President Clinton's new covenant with the family has extended the definition of "family" far more inclusively and more generously than the Christian Coalition's *Contract with the American Family*, the actual practices of the government under Clinton continue and further extend a long-standing tradition of unnecessary invasion of the lives of some families, while abandoning the desperate needs of others. Meanwhile religious liberals for the most part simply ignore family issues as such.

Who will address the real needs, particularly the economic needs, of real families? According to the Associated Press, the economic gap between the richest and poorest families in this country continues to grow, such that it now stands at $54,613 for a family of four, the highest difference among the eighteen most productive industrial countries in the world.[10] This gap notwithstanding, Congress panders to the Christian Coalition by tossing them the poor, especially poor women and children, by seeking to deny funding for abortions to low-income victims of rape and incest, and by seeking to forbid welfare funding to unwed teenagers and their babies. If the Christian Coalition has its way, Congress will demolish the Legal Services Corporation because it assists poor women seeking divorce. Furthermore, tax money may now subsidize religious education through vouchers; more and more school systems adopt mandated moments of silence; and sex education in the public schools is becoming a joke. The pro-family movement recently defeated curriculum reform in Ohio for being too humanistic. They defeated legislation in the state of Georgia that would have kept local law enforcement agencies from charging rape victims for medical tests on the grounds that it would incidentally codify law against marital rape. Opponents to the legislation claimed that the legislation violated the biblical principle that the bodies of husbands and wives belong to each other. Last but not least, the Christian Coalition, in concert with big business, seeks to dismantle environmental regulation and to render the Environmental Protection Agency even more powerless than it presently is.[11] In spite of all this damage, liberal Christians who do not agree with the Christian Coalition's program have yet to find an organized voice in the public arena, though evangelical Protestants organized by Wallis around the *Cry for Renewal* are protesting on behalf of the poor.

As Christians we should direct our concern toward the economic realities that now confront families, particularly poverty-stricken families, rather than blame the very people who are victims of these realities. Global capitalism, not feminism, is breaking up families. The median real wage for male workers has fallen steadily since 1973. For all but college-educated women in general, wages have fallen since 1989. Economist Lester Thurow attributes this decline to a number of factors. Cheap foreign labor, cheap immigration labor, the use of new technologies to replace workers, megamergers, and a disproportionate number of low-paying jobs in the service sector all contribute to the instability of families. Children have become more and more expensive to feed and to educate for longer and longer periods of time. Parents thus have strong economic incentives to abandon their children. Men, more often than women, leave their families in ever increasing numbers. For the men who abandon, this means a 73 percent increase in their standard of living. For the families abandoned, this means a 42 percent decrease in their standard of living.[12] Our present economic system, not feminism, is antithetical to family life.

The United Nations Fourth World Conference on Women, held in Beijing in the fall of 1995, sought to address, among other things, the plight of poor women, who comprise 70 percent of the world's poor, many of them primarily responsible for their children. Yet James Dobson, head of the ultra-right Focus on the Family and affiliated with the Christian Coalition, mailed out about two million fund-raising letters to constituents vilifying the conference as hostile toward the family. The letter charged Hillary Rodham Clinton, among other U.S. delegates, with killing babies, indiscriminately dispensing condoms, destroying religion, and attempting to turn all children into homosexuals. It further alleged that doctors in Chinese hospitals perform abortions in order to eat the fetuses.[13]

Concern with justice and well-being for *all* families, including future families, is a valid Christian concern. Concern for all families, however, stands in striking contrast to the vision of the Christian Coalition, the narrowness of the *Contract with the American Family*, the invasiveness and overreaction of the state at all levels, and the neglect of religious liberalism. As Christians we best manifest this concern when we seek to involve representatives from all kinds of families in the decision-making processes that ultimately affect their lives. To effect this kind of involvement, we need to get those normally excluded from the centers of power to the table and simultaneously to get the churches out into the streets, the prisons, the hospitals, and all other arenas neglected or abandoned by current social and political institutions. We need to abandon the model of mainstream and margin and imagine human society more creatively in terms of fluid coalitions among grassroots organizations within a wider global network.

Conclusion

Throughout this discussion I have tried to keep theology directly connected to practical concerns for family life and to concrete proposals to better serve families. These proposals have included both positive and negative suggestions.

I have made several proposals: church support for the kind of gang summits and local community organization backed by Wallis and Tony Campolo; the introduction of the historical and comparative study of religions into the public schools; support for interreligious dialogue; the organization of summits on the health care of children; and dispersal of copies of the United Nations Convention on the Rights of the Child directly to the congregations within the denominations for serious study and consideration. I have also urged that concerned Christians work for the development and passage of legislation that establishes and protects the rights and obligations of parents and of children in relation to one another at every level of government. Such legislation should also provide services that guarantee a safety net of economic and emotional care for children irrespective of the circumstances of their parents. Such legislation must include special, careful attention to how and under what circumstances the state may intervene into family life to protect family members at risk from others in the family. In light of this concern to strengthen and to sustain family relations, I have recommended that churches redefine the roles and responsibilities of godparents.

I have issued critical challenges on two fronts. I have challenged the approach and the programs of the Christian Coalition, particularly as represented by the *Contract with the American Family*. I have also taken issue with the practices of the government. In regard to the Christian Coalition's *Contract with the American Family* I have challenged almost every point; however, I have focused most extensively on the proposals for a religious liberties amendment and for a parental rights act. Concerning the practices of the government and irrespective of whether the politics are liberal or conservative, I have questioned at length how and under what circumstances the government has historically intervened in family life in a religious context.

I have sought throughout this discussion to define the concept *family* in ways that acknowledge the diversity of structures characteristic of contemporary family life, and I have further argued that commitment to the human family precludes all attempts to privilege certain family configurations, particularly male-dominated ones, over others. At the same time I have pointed out that commitment to the human family should not obscure real differences in circumstances and cultural values among human beings. Moreover, I have argued that poor families and family members at risk from other members within their families have immediate priority in terms of those whose needs religious communities and governmental agencies must first address. I have further urged that policy makers and legislators bring those whose needs are most dire into the political processes that generate the policies that affect their lives. In short, I have tried to make a theological case for a radically activist democratic society that protects dissent and validates differences in cultural values without fomenting division, in order to effect genuine freedom for all citizens. Nevertheless, simply voting one's conscience and campaigning for the political candidates of choice will not bring about these changes. Where then do we as Christians, insofar as we share these family values, go from here?

Our faith needs to acknowledge, to affirm, and to adopt Jesus' ambivalence toward particular family ties, as well as the implications of his tenuous relations with the authority of the state and with institutional religious authority. Insofar as the Christian churches seek to remain true to these biblical roots, they stand in tension with conventional family ties, with the state, and with the churches' own tendencies toward idolatry. For rank-and-file Christians this tension requires developing a high tolerance for complexity and ambiguity. On the one hand, Christian communities need to affirm family life in all its diversity, insofar as it sustains the well-being of all members. On the other hand, Christian communities need to challenge those structures and acts that damage family life in general and that violate particular family members. Further, even where well-being is not at risk, Christian communities must call Christians beyond their immediate family loyalties, including their religious loyalties, to minister to those who suffer injustice, wherever we find them.

This prophetic role of the churches to challenge ongoing damage, violation, and other forms of injustice emerges out of the recognition that all creatures belong to God, itself the very source of Christian liberty. Belonging to God relativizes all other authority, thereby freeing Christians to engage in the world in ways that both affirm and challenge all finite institutions. This freedom to challenge finite institutions potentially places the churches not only in tension with the family, but also in tension with the state. This prophetic role further calls the churches to accountability through ongoing, serious self-critique within and across the churches in light of God's grace. The First Amendment guarantees the liberty to worship the God to whom we belong without outside interference, including interference from Christians with whom we disagree.

As Christians we are free to involve ourselves, through the church, in sustaining healthy civic life and in struggling with the responsibilities and limits of government in meeting the needs of its people. This means both speaking out against inappropriate government intervention in family life and speaking out for appropriate intervention, as well as calling government into account for its own day-to-day role in sustaining the health, education, and welfare of all its constituents. This involvement means, moreover, struggling honestly and fairly with the differences among Christians over issues of family, state, and religion.

How, then, do Christians set about practically to work on these tasks? Miller-McLemore's idea of Christians as mothers, or the people who care, provides an excellent starting point (185–95). This care should be mutual within the confines of an actual congregation or denomination in order to prevent burnout among congregants. It should also extend beyond these boundaries to minister to the needs of outsiders, irrespective of their religious or nonreligious perspectives and without condition in regard to their politics. Thus the churches become the kind of mother who not only addresses the needs of others but gets her own needs met as well.

In regard to getting her own needs met, the local church as mother must seriously address the problems families and single people who number among her members face. Many churches are already addressing these needs in exciting ways, and surely a million creative ideas are out there among the laity, waiting to be voiced, heard, and acted on. I suggested earlier redesigning the job of godparenting. Churches might also consider creating the role of godchildren as well. As the population of this country ages, the number of elderly people who suffer abuse at the hands of badly run institutions or their own children rapidly increases. Godchildren could shoulder the task of helping those adult children who must assume financial, medical, and emotional responsibility for their parents with their decision making on behalf of the parents, as well as with the day-to-day tasks involved in caring for them.[14] Godchildren might also adopt single elderly people and those whose children have abandoned them, in order to perform the tasks that need to be done to ease their twilight years. Ideas like this need to circulate among congregations.

In regard to outreach beyond the boundaries of both the local churches and their respective denominations, many creative programs exist in support of family needs which the churches are undertaking, ranging from involvement with Habitat for Humanity and shelters for the homeless to the ten-point program organized by a coalition of Boston churches for citywide church mobilization.[15] We have nevertheless neglected two areas of urgent concern. We have yet to realize adequately the extent to which care for the earth in an ecologically threatened age is truly a family value. We also have yet to grasp the full implications of living in an electronic age for radical democratic participation in a religiously plural, secular society.

In regard to ecological concerns, many churches have involved themselves in various movements to overcome the pollution of the earth. Such churches participate in programs to "reduce, reuse, and recycle" waste. They conduct study groups on stewardship of the earth. Some denominational seminaries are "greening" both their campuses and their curricula. Denominations fund experiments in ecologically sound living throughout the country as well. Councils and committees meet to struggle with ecojustice. More and more Christians are eating less and less meat. More and more Christians are using the credit card and long-distance services of Working Assets, a politically activist company that agitates for ecojustice with Congress and the White House.[16]

Few churches, however, have undertaken the difficult struggle of confronting industries whose pollution presently destroys the lives of whole families from birth to death. So, for example, Roman Catholic nuns take on companies who chemically pollute the water along the border of the United States with Mexico, thereby poisoning the drinking water of *maquiladora* workers whose children are increasingly born with defects like spina bifida. Meanwhile, other denominations duck these issues in deference to their constituencies who are entrepreneurs engaged in some of this injustice. Families on both sides of the border are the direct beneficiaries of the environmental damage done here. As Christians we need to conceive and to address much more concretely the implications of this kind of environmental damage to family life.[17]

As people who care, who concern ourselves with building community today, we most of all need to think community itself differently. We need to organize both across Christian denominations and with communities of very different faiths. In the past the model for community has assumed face-to-face contact with like-minded people, organized fairly permanently around a common cause. This model is not about to disappear, but it is undergoing drastic modification at the hands of electronic technology. For example, forming coalitions with diverse religious and secular groups through electronic communication allows more and different voices to be heard. This diversity can further be nurtured and preserved on-line through education and through formal dialogue among members of all faiths, whether religious or nonreligious. The technology already exists to make this kind of organizing, education, and dialogue cheaper and easier than ever before. In short, through electronic communication we already possess the means to build stronger and better communities to nurture particularly those families at risk.

Access to the Internet provides opportunities for fluid, loosely organized coalitions among diverse groups of people who may never see each other face to face, but who in perhaps more transitory ways nevertheless share common causes. Most denominations and activist groups from Presbyterians to Sojourners and the Christian Coalition have home pages on the World Wide Web, as well as electronic mail by which to communicate directly. Roman Catholics have set up on-line capacity in order to engage in direct and ongoing conversation with one another. This flurry of activity constitutes only the smallest beginning of what is to come. Why are we not talking with each other directly about those issues that matter most across our denominations and beyond our various Christian faiths? Imagine what it would be like to create on-line "rooms" for dialogue and debate of family issues and to arrange for a "meeting" between Reed and Wallis, or between Weber and Miller-McLemore, into which the rest of us might have input.

The greatest untapped resource in this area of community building, however, consists in bringing poor people directly into such conversations. Christians need to assume responsibility for getting this kind of technology and the opportunity it provides for grassroots organization and political activism directly into the hands of those whose voices are most often silenced and ignored.

For example, seventy-seven-year-old R. G. Bouchum of Longview, Texas, recently corresponded by electronic mail with his daughter in Fairbanks, Alaska. Thanks to the Texas Literacy Council, he started learning to read and write at the age of seventy-four. He now manages Windows software and America Online programs with relative ease. According to the Associated Press, his daughter, deeply moved by the communication, noted that in her forty-eight years she had never received written correspondence from her father.[18] Shouldn't support for this kind of connection among loved ones be at least partly what family values are all about?

Through the churches Christians need to be at the forefront of fostering computer literacy and access to the Internet for poor people. We need to be working with funding agencies, as well as using our own budgets, to provide volunteer teachers, personal computers, and on-line services in shelters for the homeless and the abused, in the public libraries, and in the common spaces of our church buildings. Thus the people to whom we minister could learn the skills they need and have access to the equipment necessary to restore lost relationship within their families and to bring them into the political processes that shape their lives. Precisely at this point we shall need most to listen carefully, to remain open, and to relinquish the need to control.

Unless and until we hear these voices speak in *their* words, there can be no real justice for families, nor can there be genuine democracy for us all. We find ourselves today in the midst of conversations and struggles begun "in the beginning," older than the birth of Jesus himself. We stand now at a far cry even from the Palestinian Jewish teacher who, long after the "beginning," went on the road that gets people who call themselves Christian to God. As people who by God's grace seek to be faithful to Jesus' vision, insofar as we can apprehend it, we are nevertheless caught up in this cry, echoing down through the ages. It is a cry for connection, for freedom, for renewal.

Notes

Introduction

1. Mary Farrell, the godmother of my nephew Heath, took this photograph.
2. See "A Time for Healing," in *And the Angels Wept: From the Pulpits of Oklahoma City after the Bombing*, ed. Marsha Brock Bishop and David P. Polk (St. Louis: Chalice Press, 1995), 50–52.
3. Ralph Reed, *Mainstream Values Are No Longer Politically Incorrect: The Emerging Faith Factor in American Politics* (Dallas: Word Publishing, 1994). Hereafter references to this work are given in parentheses in the text. See also *Christian Coalition Presents The Contract with the American Family*, available on the Christian Coalition home page through World Wide Web. The address is: http://www.cc.org (downloaded June 1995). The Christian Coalition may be reached at 1-800-325-4746.
4. Jim Wallis, *The Soul of Politics: A Practical and Prophetic Vision for Change* (Maryknoll, N.Y.: Orbis Books, 1994; New York: New Press, 1994). Hereafter references to this work are given in parentheses in the text. See also *The Cry for Renewal*, available on Sojourners home page through World Wide Web. The address is http://www/sojourners.com/sojourners/home.html (downloaded July 1995). Sojourners may be reached at 1-800-714-7474.

Chapter 1: Images of the Family

1. See, for example, *May v. Cooperman*, 572 F. supp. 1561, 14 Ed. Law Rep. 456. (1983) 44. Unless otherwise specified, all legal documentation comes from the Westlaw data base, as leased by Trinity University's

Elizabeth Coates Maddox Library. On grounds too technical to explore here I disagree with the court's judgment that such practices do not establish a state religion.

2. Theologian H. Richard Niebuhr argues that faith is a universal condition of human existence. He defines faith as trust in and loyalty to a center of value. The center of value may range from religious to secular in character. Thus, just as Jews place their faith in God as a center of value, so scientists place their faith in the ultimate knowability of natural law. See his *Radical Monotheism and Western Culture with Supplementary Essays* (New York: Harper & Row, 1960), esp. 16–23 and 78–89.

3. Stephanie Coontz, *The Way We Never Were: American Families and the Nostalgia Trap* (New York: Basic Books, 1992).

4. Stu Weber, *Tender Warrior: God's Intention for Man* (Sisters, Oreg.: Multnomah Books, 1993).

5. For an alternative to fundamentalist interpretations, see Carol A. Newsom and Sharon H. Ringe, eds., *The Women's Bible Commentary* (Louisville, Ky.: Westminster/John Knox Press, 1992). See also Elisabeth Schüssler Fiorenza, "Women in the Early Christian Movement," in *Womanspirit Rising: A Feminist Reader in Religion*, ed. Carol P. Christ and Judith Plaskow (New York: Harper & Row, 1979), 84–92.

6. See respectively John Updike, *Roger's Version* (New York: Alfred A. Knopf, 1986), and Nathaniel Hawthorne, *The Scarlet Letter* (Boston: Houghton Mifflin Co., 1960).

7. Jane Smiley, *A Thousand Acres* (New York: Alfred A. Knopf, 1991).

8. See Toni Morrison, *Beloved* (New York: Alfred A. Knopf, 1987). Hereafter reference to this work is given in parentheses in the text. See also Marsha Jean Darling, "A Conversation with Toni Morrison," in *The Women's Review of Books*, 5/6 (March 1988).

9. See also Toni Morrison, *Song of Solomon* (New York: Alfred A. Knopf, 1977).

10. Daniel Patrick Moynihan's *The Negro Family: The Case for National Action* provides the earliest noteworthy example of what has since become a national pastime, namely, maligning African American women for their poverty. Printed in full in *The Moynihan Report and the Politics of Controversy*, ed. Lee Rainwater and William Yancey (Cambridge, Mass.: MIT Press, 1967), 39–124.

11. This conception of faith obviously owes a major debt to the theology of H. Richard Niebuhr, particularly *Radical Monotheism and Western Culture with Supplementary Essays*, esp. 16–23. At this point in history, however, I am somewhat more concerned with faith in relation to religious plurality, whereas the historical circumstances of Niebuhr's time required that he give primary attention to universality.

12. On the relation between faith and the widening of one's affections, see Richard R. Niebuhr, *Experiential Religion* (New York: Harper & Row, 1972).

Chapter 2: Family as the People of God

1. The current controversy surrounding family values involves far many more issues than this discussion can take into account. Furthermore, the actual content of the values themselves and the particular conflicts associated with them will emerge in the discussion of how family values relate specifically to issues of gender and to constitutional rights. I wish to focus here on two points.
2. See "American Values: Life, Liberty, and Try Pursuing a Bit of Tolerance Too," *The Economist* 5 (September 1992), and "Family Values: The Bargain Breaks," *The Economist* 26 (December 1992).
3. *White House Conference on Families—Families and Human Needs—Handbook* (Baltimore, 1980), 2.
4. Pat Robertson, 1992 fund-raising letter to prevent passage of an Equal Rights Amendment to the Iowa state constitution, also cited in "Backlash: A Roundtable Discussion," *Journal of Feminist Studies in Religion*, contributors Beverly Harrison, Carter Heyward, Mary E. Hunt, Starhawk, Anne L. Barstow, and Paula M. Cooey, 10/1 (1994): 91.
5. See Walter Rauschenbusch, *A Theology for the Social Gospel* (Nashville: Abingdon Press, 1945).

Chapter 3: Thinking Difference Differently

1. How to interpret biblical narrative and the authority of such interpretations depend on assumptions that theologians and Bible scholars presently dispute. A discussion of hermeneutics in the context of a radically pluralistic democracy in a postmodern era falls outside the limits of the subject of family values, although conflict over family values connects directly to and stands in reciprocal relation with conflict over biblical authority.
2. My interpretation is particularly indebted to Phyllis Trible, "Genesis 2—3 Reread," in *Womanspirit Rising: A Feminist Reader in Religion*, ed. Carol P. Christ and Judith Plaskow (New York: Harper & Row, 1979), 74–83. Hereafter references are given in parentheses in the text.
3. See, for example, Augustine, *On the Trinity*, Book XII, trans. Stephen McKenna, C.SS.R. (Washington, D.C.: Catholic University of America Press, 1963), 343–68, and Karl Barth, "Freedom in Fellowship," *Church Dogmatics III/4: The Doctrine of Creation* (Edinburgh: T. & T. Clark, 1961), sec. 54, part 1, pp. 116–240.
4. This interpretation characterizes many Jewish and Christian mystical writings. For example, see the interleaved Bible of Jonathan Edwards at the Beinecke Library, Yale University, New Haven, Connecticut.
5. *Calvin: Institutes of the Christian Religion*, ed. John T. McNeill, trans. Ford Lewis Battles (Philadelphia: Westminster Press, 1960), 1.6–10, esp. 7.
6. Augustine employs a similar strategy for mediating biblical interpretation in *On Christian Doctrine*, trans. with intro. by D. W. Robertson, Jr. (New York: Liberal Arts Press, 1958).

7. Robert Bly, *Iron John: A Book about Men* (Reading, Mass.: Addison-Wesley Publishing Co., 1990).

8. See Bonnie Miller-McLemore, *Also a Mother: Work and Family as Theological Dilemma* (Nashville: Abingdon Press, 1994). Hereafter references to this work are given in parentheses in the text.

9. For Erikson's definition of *generativity*, see Erik H. Erikson, *Insight and Responsibility: Lectures on the Ethical Implications of Psychoanalytic Insight* (New York: W. W. Norton & Co., 1964).

10. John Calvin, *Commentary on the First Book of Moses, Called Genesis*, trans. John King (Edinburgh: Calvin Translation Society, 1847–50), 159.

11. My own personal preference is for hiding from God in fear. It makes sense to me that up until that point, Adam and Eve could have worked things out with God. The sin was not to trust that God and their relation to God could overcome even disobedience and betrayal. Sin originates in hiding out of fear from the one source that can heal and reconcile human mistakes and breaches of relationship. Fear in this case, rather than reverence for God, reflects human distrust of God.

12. It is interesting to note that the translators who produced the Jerusalem Bible translate this passage slightly differently. According to this translation, the woman's desire shall be for her husband, but he shall "lord it" over her. On the face of things, this translation restricts male control to sexual practices rather than the more general "rule" explicated in the New Revised Standard Version. In which case whether God is cursing the first couple or simply pointing out the consequences of their actions, God is in neither case validating sexism or patriarchy. Rather, one gets the sense the woman will possess a lusty sexual appetite for the man, which he will frustrate by sexually withholding himself or by sexually controlling her in other ways, just as the land will in turn withhold its bounty from him.

13. Just as an aside, one way to read the text presupposes that the human couple had always been vulnerable to death. Though God threatens death, should Adam eat the fruit, this does not necessarily mean that the first humans would have escaped death forever, had they never eaten from the tree. Quite the contrary, it could simply mean that the fruit would instantly kill them upon eating it, thereby ending any possibility for a human future. In short, the threat could be interpreted as a threat of *untimely* death. Thus, the couple's sin does not introduce death into the world, a condition that was already in effect by implication; furthermore, in light of sin, death is a mercy.

14. Pat Robertson, 1992 fund-raising letter to prevent passage of an Equal Rights Amendment to the Iowa state constitution. See chapter 2, note 4.

15. Quoted in the *San Antonio Express-News* in "Gingrich vows House vote on new moral blueprint," May 18, 1995, 7A.

16. See, for example, Carol J. Adams, *Neither Man Nor Beast: Feminism and the Defense of Animals* (New York: Continuum, 1994), and Rosemary

Radford Ruether, *Gaia and God: An Ecofeminist Theology of Earth Healing* (San Francisco: Harper, 1992).

17. Hal Lindsey with C. C. Carlson, *The Late Great Planet Earth* (Grand Rapids: Zondervan Publishing House, 1970).

Chapter 4: The Moment of Silence

1. From the Declaration of Independence, July 4, 1776, first paragraph.
2. Rather than using both masculine and feminine pronouns to indicate inclusivity (a practice that can become extremely burdensome) I vary the gender throughout the text generically. For example: "Anyone who wishes may use her pencil instead of her pen. However, sometimes when he uses his pencil instead of his pen, his writing is too light for me to see."
3. I am indebted to my editor, Jon Berquist, for reminding me of these further economic implications of restricting the vote to property owners.
4. The Bill of Rights, First Amendment to the Constitution of the United States of America.
5. Thomas Jefferson makes this reference in a letter to the Danbury Baptist Association, written January 1, 1802. Justice William H. Rehnquist cites it in *Grand Rapids v. Ball*, 105 S.Ct. 2479 (1985).
6. See *Reynolds v. United States*, 98 U.S. 145 (1878) and Donald L. Drakeman, *Church-State Constitutional Issues* (New York: Greenwood Press, 1991), 3.
7. *Engel v. Vitale*, 370 U.S. 421 at 430, 432.
8. *Lemon v. Kurtzman*, 403 U.S. 602.
9. *Tinker v. Des Moines Independent School District* 89 S.Ct. 733 (1969).
10. *May v. Cooperman*, 572 F. Supp. 1561 (1983).
11. For a fuller discussion of the history of court attitudes, as well as decisions in regard to religious observance, see Ronald B. Flowers, *That Godless Court? Supreme Court Decisions on Church-State Relationships* (Louisville, Ky.: Westminster John Knox Press, 1994).
12. The Court has on occasion drawn a strict distinction between belief and ritual that reflects a Protestant bias. So, for example, the Court has stipulated that one may believe what one wishes, but one may not ritually act on those beliefs if they violate secular laws. For many religious traditions, not to engage in ritual acts that substantiate belief is to violate one's religion and may place the believer at risk of various possible eternal or temporary punishments. While there may be reasons of public interest for prohibiting certain kinds of ritual actions like human sacrifice, other ritual activity like ingesting peyote as practiced by the Native American Church in no way threatens the public interest. See *Oregon v. Smith*, 494 U.S. 872 (1990).
13. First proposal of *Contract with the American Family*.
14. See, for example, *Lee v. Weisman*, 112 S.Ct. 2649 (1992) and *Doe v. Duncanville*, 994 F. 2d 160 (1993).

15. President Clinton, quoted in the *San Antonio Express-News*, July 13, 1995, 1A.

16. "Administration issues guidelines on school prayer," *New York Times* Service, *San Antonio Express-News*, August 26, 1995, 1A, 11A.

Chapter 5: On Behalf of the Children

1. See Marie Ashe and Naomi Cahn, "Child Abuse: A Problem for Feminist Theory," *Texas Journal of Women and the Law* 2/1 (1993): 75–112, and *De Shaney v. Winnebago*, S.Ct. 489 US 189 (1989); also *Supreme Court Reports*, vol. 109, 998 and *Lawyers Edition*, vol. 103, 249. I am indebted to Milner S. Ball, Caldwell Professor of Constitutional Law at the University of Georgia, for alerting me to this case.

2. See respectively, Hillary Rodham, "Children under the Law," in *The Rights of Children* (Cambridge, Mass.: Harvard Educational Review, 1974) 1–28, and "Children's Rights: A Legal Perspective," in *Children's Rights: A Contemporary Perspective*, ed. Patricia A. Vardin and Ilene N. Brody (New York: Teachers College Press, Columbia University, 1979), 21–36.

3. For the text of the treaty, see Lawrence J. LeBlanc, *The Convention on the Rights of the Child*, Appendix C (Lincoln: University of Nebraska Press, 1995), 293–316. Hereafter reference to this work is given in parentheses in the text. For the Christian Coalition's reasons for opposing the treaty, see the *Contract with the American Family*, "Protecting Parental Rights."

4. See, for example, Malfrid Grude Flekkoy, *A Voice for Children: Speaking Out as Their Ombudsman* (London: Jessica Kingsley Publishers, 1991). Hereafter references to this work are given in parentheses in the text.

5. Pat Robertson's ceaseless vilification of Hillary Rodham Clinton serves as a prime example.

6. *Davis v. Beason*, 133 U.S. 333, 10 S.Ct. 299 (1890).

7. *Prince v. Massachusetts*, 321 U.S. 158, 64 S.Ct. 438 (1944).

8. See *Commonwealth of Massachusetts v. David R. Twitchell*, 416 Mass. 114, 617 N.E. 2d 609 (1993), and Andrew Skolnick, "Religious Exemptions to Child Neglect Laws Still Being Passed despite Convictions of Parents," *Journal of the American Medical Association*, September 12, 1990, 1226.

9. James R. Lewis, ed., *From the Ashes: Making Sense out of Waco*, (Lanham, Md.: Rowman & Littlefield, 1994).

10. Barbara Krantowitz, "The Messiah of Waco," *Newsweek* 121/11 (March 15, 1993): 56(1).

11. Diane McCormick and Mark England, "A Long, Troubled Road Led Branch Davidians to Waco," *Waco Tribune-Herald*, February 27, 1993, A10.

12. Mary Gotschall, "A Marriage Made in Hell," *National Review*, April 4, 1994, 57(4).

13. Daniel Wattenberg, "Gunning for Koresh," *American Spectator* 26 (August 1993): 36, 37.

14. Diana R. Fuentes, "Girl describes how Koresh raped her when she was ten," *San Antonio Express-News*, July 21, 1995, 1A.
15. See respectively, Diana R. Fuentes, "ATF agent says he cried on finding his warning didn't halt Waco raid," *San Antonio Express-News*, July 25, 1995, 1A, 4A, and Fuentes, "Davidians' lawyers call for harder look at the FBI," *San Antonio Express-News*, July 26, 1995, 1A, 8A.
16. For the best study of Waco done to date, see Eugene V. Gallagher and Jim Tabor, *Why Waco: Cults and the Battle for Religious Freedom in America* (Berkeley: University of California Press, 1995). See also Dick J. Reavis, *The Ashes of Waco: An Investigation* (New York: Simon & Schuster, 1995).
17. Her father and mother were divorced, and her father, not a Branch Davidian, lived elsewhere. Fuentes, "ATF agent says."
18. In the case of the fundamentalist preacher, see "Minister arrested on child abuse charges" and "Preacher vows to fight state over children put in custody," both in the *San Antonio Express-News*, front-page stories respectively December 1 and December 8, 1988. On the beheading, see "Father flees with son's severed head," *San Antonio Express-News*, July 23, 1995. The man who molested his stepdaughter is Susan Smith's stepfather. Susan Smith was recently convicted of murdering her two sons. See "Mother in South Carolina Convicted of Murdering Her Two Sons," *New York Times*, July 23, 1995, 1A, 20A. See also Molly Ivins, "Temper remedy of 'the family,' " *San Antonio Express-News*, September 12, 1995, 5B.
19. *Contract with the American Family*, "Protecting Parental Rights."
20. See note 1.

Chapter 6: Building Community Today

1. There are, of course, admonitions regulating family relations in male-dominated ways along biological lines in some of the Pauline epistles (disputed in regard to authorship, by the way) and likewise in the pastoral epistles. These injunctions tend to go hand in hand with the regulation of the behavior of slaves and are no more relevant and binding on Christians today than the codes governing slavery. See, for example, the household codes cited in chapter 1 and the *Women's Bible Commentary*.
2. Given a long, complicated, and ugly history of Christian anti-Judaism and anti-Semitism, I think it very important to emphasize that, to the extent that Jesus challenged religious authority, he did so as an insider, as one who sought to live Torah, not as one who stood outside Judaism, nor one who rejected it, nor even as one who was rejected by all Jews.
3. For a fuller development of these points, see Eleanor McLaughlin, "The Christian Past: Does It Hold a Future for Women?" in *Womanspirit Rising: A Feminist Reader in Religion*, ed. Carol P. Christ and Judith Plaskow (New York: Harper & Row, 1979), 93–119.
4. See Jonathan Edwards, *Images or Shadows of Divine Things*, ed. with in-

tro. by Perry Miller (New Haven, Conn.: Yale University Press, 1948), 114–15.

5. Karl Barth, *Church Dogmatics*, I/2.17, *The Doctrine of the Word of God*, "The Revelation of God as the Abolition of Religion" (Edinburgh: T. & T. Clark, 1956), 280–361, and *The Constitution of the Presbyterian Church (U.S.A.)*, Part I: *Book of Confessions*, The Theological Declaration of Barmen, 8.01–8.28, particularly 8.11-.12.

6. H. Richard Niebuhr, *The Meaning of Revelation* (New York: Macmillan Co., 1941), 7, 10, 133.

7. I am grateful to Professor Frank Garcia for his helpful comments, though I am solely responsible for the position taken here.

8. I am grateful to George Khushf, assistant professor in the philosophy department at the University of South Carolina, for a fruitful conversation (August 10, 1995) in which we struggled with what it would mean to create such a space.

9. In *The Meaning of Revelation*, H. Richard Niebuhr notes, "Revelation is not the development of our religious ideas but their continuous conversion. God's self-disclosure is that permanent revolution in our religious life by which all religious truths are painfully transformed and all religious behavior transfigured by repentance and new faith" (133).

10. "Study finds U.S. has wide rich-poor gap," *San Antonio Express-News*, August 15, 1995, 6B.

11. Tom Teepen, "Religious right gaining in statehouses," *Comment, San Antonio Express-News*, August 15, 1995, 4B.

12. Lester C. Thurow, "Companies Merge; Families Break Up," *New York Times*, September 3, 1995, 11E.

13. Susan Yerkes, "Women still have a long way to go," *San Antonio Express-News*, September 3, 1995, 1H.

14. The realization that children eventually relate to their parents as relative equals and still later assume responsibility for them has intriguing implications for how we think about God as parent. That we are all somebody's children or more generally God's children does not mean we have to remain throughout our lives in arrested development in relation either to our parents or to God.

15. Listed in full in Wallis, *The Soul of Politics*, 224–26.

16. For information on both long-distance and credit card services, Working Assets may be reached at 1-800-788-8588.

17. For more information, the Coalition for Justice in the Maquiladoras may be reached at 3120 W. Ashby, San Antonio, TX 78228.

18. "Father goes from illiteracy to e-mail," *San Antonio Express-News*, August 18, 1995, 18A.